D0754443

EVERY
———
LAST
———
TIE

DISCARD

EVERY

LAST

TIE

THE STORY OF
THE UNABOMBER AND
HIS FAMILY

DAVID KACZYNSKI

AFTERWORD BY JAMES L. KNOLL IV, MD

DUKE UNIVERSITY PRESS DURHAM AND LONDON 2016

Library of Congress Cataloging-in-Publication Data
Kaczynski, David, [date] author.
Every last tie : the story of the Unabomber and his family / David Kaczynski.
pages cm
Includes bibliographical references and index.
ISBN 978-0-8223-5980-7 (hardcover : alk. paper)
ISBN 978-0-8223-7500-5 (e-book)
1. Kaczynski, Theodore John, [date] 2. Bombers (Terrorists) —
Family relationships — United States. 3. Capital punishment —
Moral and ethical aspects — United States. I. Title.
HV6248.K235K33 2016
364.152′3092 — dc23
[B]
2015019794

ALL PHOTOGRAPHS IN THE GALLERY ARE COURTESY OF THE AUTHOR.
COVER ART: TEDDY WITH PARAKEET AND DAVID, 1952

— *For Sylvia Dombek* —

RETURN

Hard to believe
that the past is
completely gone, not
a closed room that
we might one day
reenter accidentally,
without anticipation,
the same way we
came in before.

Then how can we
fail to experience
the room's emptiness,
the lack of walls,
the weather?

—DAVID KACZYNSKI

CONTENTS

Photo gallery appears after page 60.

PREFACE

IN THE LATE SUMMER OF 1995, my wife, Linda Patrik, sat me down for a serious talk. She put her hand on my knee. I could hear stress in her voice.

"David, don't be angry with me," she began. I expected her to tell me about something that was bothering her, perhaps some habit of mine that she found irritating. Linda could be blunt. I'd learned to appreciate her direct approach. It didn't leave me guessing what my life partner thought or needed.

"Has it ever occurred to you, even as a remote possibility," she continued, "that your brother might be the Unabomber?"

At first I wasn't sure I'd heard her right. "What?"

She repeated her question, and I felt a mixture of consternation and defensiveness. This was my only brother she was talking about!

I knew Ted was mentally ill, plagued with afflictive emotions. I'd worried about him for years. I'd entertained unanswered questions about his estrangement from the family. But it never had occurred to me that Ted was capable of violence. So far as I knew, he'd never *been* violent.

At that time, the hunt for the Unabomber was the longest-running, most expensive criminal investigation in the history of the FBI. Over seventeen years, the shadowy Unabomber had sent through the mail or placed in public areas sixteen explosive devices that had claimed three lives and injured dozens more, some seriously. Within the last year, the Unabomber had killed two people — Gilbert Murray, a forestry industry lobbyist, and Thomas Mosser, an advertising executive. The Los Angeles airport had recently been shut down after it received a threatening letter from the Unabomber. Meanwhile, the Unabomber had sent a seventy-eight-page manifesto to the *New York Times* and the *Washington Post* and demanded that it be published, or else more bombs would be sent to unsuspecting victims.

At first I assumed Linda had let her imagination run away with her. She pointed out that although the manifesto had not yet been published, it was being described by media sources as a critique of modern technology. She knew my brother had an obsession with the negative effects of technology. She mentioned that one bomb had been placed at the University of California at Berkeley, where Ted was once a mathematics professor.

"That was thirty years ago!" I countered. "Berkeley is a hotbed for radicals. Besides, Ted hates to travel. He has no money."

"But we loaned him money, didn't we?"

I didn't like the way the conversation was developing. The human mind can take any fixed idea and patch together evidence to support it. That's what I thought was going on. But I wondered why Linda had focused such attention on my brother.

"If the Unabomber's manifesto is ever published, would you at least read it and tell me honestly what you think?" she pleaded.

Well, I could do that much. In fact, reading the manifesto might be the best way to allay Linda's fear. At that stage, I wasn't capable of imagining that the Unabomber and my mixed-up brother could be the same person. I'd had extensive correspondence with Ted; I knew how he thought and how he wrote. Surely after reading the manifesto I'd be able to say to Linda, "It's not him!"

A month later, when I read the newly published manifesto, *Industrial Society and Its Future*, I found that I couldn't in good faith tell Linda it wasn't written by my brother. Nor could I tell myself that it *was* written by him. I'd been an English major, a lover of literature. I assumed that a person's writing would be as distinctive and identifiable as their voice. But if it was indeed Ted's "voice" that I heard in the Unabomber's manifesto, it came to me muffled through thick layers of dread and denial.

Over the next two months, we read the manifesto repeatedly and made careful comparisons with letters that Ted had sent me over the years from his one-room cabin in rural Montana. Sometimes I thought I was projecting my worry, seeing what I feared to see, since Linda had planted a strong suggestion in my mind. At other times I thought I might be in denial, unable to see the painful truth because I lacked the wherewithal to deal with it.

Yet the day came when I finally acknowledged to Linda that she might be right. "Hon, I think there might be a 50–50 chance that Ted wrote the manifesto."

Now our question *Is Ted the Unabomber?* led me to a seemingly endless series of other questions and concerns: *What will this do to my brother? What will this do to my mother?* (I thought they both might die.) *What will this do to us—to Linda and me? What kind of life will we have if it turns out that my brother really is the Unabomber?* And, of course, the most urgent and compelling question: *What should we do with our suspicion that we know the identity of the most wanted criminal in America, a serial killer?*

IN THE AFTERMATH OF Ted's arrest, in April 1996, our home in Schenectady, New York, was surrounded by the media. They hounded us. They somehow gained access to our bank records. They dug through our garbage. They called our unlisted numbers. They besieged our friends and relatives with interview requests. A picture of our little cabin in southwestern Texas showed up in the *New York Times*. The same U.S. government that had promised us complete confidentiality turned into a leaky sieve of information about the Kaczynskis. It felt as if we had not a shred of privacy or dignity left.

At first it looked like the media were trying to dig up dirt in answer to their questions. *What kind of family would produce the Unabomber? What kind of person would turn in his own brother?*

The early stories were floundering, scattered. A late-night comedian dubbed me the "Una-snitch." But eventually a narrative began to take shape. The *New York Times*, in an editorial titled "His Brother's Keeper," characterized me as a moral hero, someone willing to exchange family loyalty and personal happiness for the lives of people he didn't know. The press calmed down and decided to more or less respect our boundaries. Linda and I soon embarked on a new and equally desperate mission: to try to save my brother from the death penalty.

FOR ALL THE MANY invasions of our privacy, the media never truly "saw" us. The emerging story was reductionist, flat, even somewhat trite in its characterization of the two brothers, one bad, one good. Linda's crucial role was first downplayed and then eliminated from the narrative entirely.

If the media really wanted to identify a moral hero in our saga, it could have discovered heroism in a couple rather than in an individual. Or it could have discovered that, far from being the leader of a righteous quest for truth, I was a reluctant follower. The leader of the righteous quest was Linda, who probably had to assume that role, considering my deep attachment to my brother. But these truths are complex, incompatible with the media's need to tell a simple tale pitched to readers' expectations.

The purpose of this book is not to set the record straight. Rather, my intention is to tell the one story that I'm uniquely situated to tell by exploring my memories of the family I was born into—a family I see as both unusual and typical. The more I delve into these memories, the more clearly I see that I am made of my relationships, and the more deeply I appreciate our profound interconnectedness within the human family.

The memoir that follows is a contemplation inspired and energized by a mixture of loving memories and painful outcomes. May it be of some benefit!

< CHAPTER 1 >

MISSING PARTS

I'LL START WITH THE PREMISE that a brother shows you who you
are — and who you are not. He's an image of the self at one remove,
but also a representation of the other.

In a universe of unlimited spatial and temporal dimensions, you
are brought together with your brother in a unique and specific con-
sanguinity. You come from the same womb. Your family has a certain
flavor and smell unlike any other. It has an ethos, perhaps even a my-
thology all its own.

You are a "we" with your brother before you are a "we" with any
other. Even your parents' "we" can be turned against you.

Your brother, if there are only two of you, is your first peer, thus
your model for later relationships.

When your brother ventures out in the world, he represents you.
If he is older, he may be your only way of being and appearing vicariously in a world that you are not yet allowed to enter. In this sense

he represents the possibility of your own future, the widening of your social presence. Your pride in your brother is, in part, egoistic projection.

In relationship to your brother, you also learn about your limitations and about personal boundaries: the things you do less well, the meaning of "belonging" as a noun, the need to compete for attention, the space that opens up for you only after it's been vacated by your brother. Especially if you are the younger one, you only begin to own yourself, to develop a fully independent identity, in your brother's absence. But his absence may haunt your aloneness.

I grew up with the idea that as brothers we are allowed and even meant to fight with each other, until someone attacks one of us. Then we will turn in unison on the attacker as one force redoubled. The older brother protects the younger with his fists and his power. But the younger brother protects the older with his admiration and love. It should be obvious who bears the greater responsibility.

In expansive affirmation, some men address other men as "brother." To designate a special friendship, or to invoke community and intimacy within a group, we use the brother formula as a foundational myth of male fellowship.

My brother, Ted Kaczynski, once sent an airline executive a bomb concealed in a hollowed-out copy of a book with the intriguing title *Ice Brothers*.

I DON'T REMEMBER A time when I wasn't aware that my brother was "special"—a tricky word that can mean either above or below average, or completely off the scale. Ted, seven and a half years older, was special because he was so intelligent. In the Kaczynski family, intelligence carried high value.

In the late 1950s, the time of Sputnik and the space race, intelligence (especially technical and scientific intelligence) assumed even greater cultural and political resonance. Ted was a "brain" to school-age children in our working-class neighborhood, where the word conferred status but also a vague stigma, since being too intelligent was linked to maladjustment, and most kids wanted to fit in.

As a young child beginning to gauge social perceptions, I thought of my brother as smart, independent, and principled. I heard myself described by our neighbors and aunts and uncles as charming, happy, and affectionate — as if those were traits to be remarked on in a child. Even at a tender age, I sensed that adults contrasted me with my brother. Heck, anyone could be the way I was; it required no effort on my part. But not everyone could be smart, independent, and principled like my big brother. Given a choice, I would gladly have embraced Ted's persona and relinquished my own. I wanted to be like Ted.

However, I distinguished myself from my brother through my interest in sports — especially baseball. One summer day, a slightly older boy in the neighborhood loaned me a glove and taught me how to play catch. Soon he was showing me his prize collection of baseball cards, asking, "Who's your best player?"

I was embarrassed to say that I didn't know the names of any big-league players. Out of the corner of my eye, I picked out a name on a card among the many my friend had spread out on the grass.

"Jim Rivera," I said.

"Oh," said my friend, "'Jungle Jim.' Yeah, I like him, too."

Later that day, I reported to my brother that Jungle Jim Rivera was my "best" baseball player. Teddy was quick to correct me. "Davy, you should say 'favorite' not 'best,'" he said. "And why, might I ask, is Jungle Jim Rivera your favorite baseball player?"

I should have known that Teddy would request a reason. Opinions, I had learned, should be based on reasoning.

"I don't know," I said, feeling slightly abashed. "I guess I just like him." At this, Teddy shook his head ruefully.

TED COULD BE CRITICAL, but he could also be kind. When I was about three, our family moved from a dingy duplex in Chicago's Back of the Yards neighborhood (the Yards being the famous Chicago stockyards) to a house in Evergreen Park, a new working-class suburb on the city's southwest side. It was our first house. When summer came, I used to delight in pushing open the screen door and going out to play in our spacious backyard. It never rained that summer (in my memory, at least). I met other boys and girls my own age. I was discovering a new world and having a ball. The only frustration came when I tried to reenter the house, because I was too short to reach the door handle to pull open the screen door. I would often stand on the back patio—a tiny exile—calling for someone, Mom or Dad or Ted, to let me in.

One day I saw Ted fiddling with something at the back door. He was ten or eleven at the time but always an ingenious person. To this day, it mesmerizes me to watch someone drawing or performing some careful manual task, which I ascribe to my early interest in my brother's activities. He had taken a spool of thread from Mom's sewing kit, and a hammer and a nail from Dad's tool kit in the basement. I watched as he removed the last remnant of thread from the spool, leaving only the bare spool. Then he inserted the nail through the hole in the center of the spool and hammered it onto the lower part of the wooden screen door. When he was finished, he said, "Dave, see if this works!" All of a sudden it dawned on me what he had done: he'd crafted a makeshift door handle for me.

Even after I grew taller and no longer needed it, the spool remained attached to the door for some time—a lingering reminder of my brother's kindness. Tender memories like this one (and there were more than a few) soothe the stings that inevitably come in a sibling relationship. Growing up, I never doubted my brother's fundamental loyalty and love or felt the slightest insecurity in his presence.

Which is not to say that I always felt worthy in his presence. It never seemed a challenge to win our parents' approval. Although humble about their own virtues and accomplishments, Mom and Dad seemed to glory in their two boys. I'm sure it was Ted who first clued me in that Mom and Dad's approval ratings were not objective. He sometimes faulted me, too, for being overly subjective. I remember asking him once, "Aren't we lucky that we have the best parents in the world?" He replied, "You can't prove that."

Sometimes I suspected Ted was judging me, even when he said nothing. I wondered if I had done something wrong that I wasn't aware of. Once when he caught me in a fib, he said, "You liar!" and stalked off in contempt. I worried that I had disappointed him terribly, perhaps beyond hope of redemption. Later, when he said nothing about the incident, I found myself studying his face trying to detect some change, but never able to penetrate the veil covering his inner thoughts and feelings.

Although I had placed Ted on a pedestal—wanting to emulate his intellectual accomplishments, bragging to my fourth-grade buddies when he went to Harvard on a scholarship at sixteen—there was another part of me that sensed he was not completely OK.

I was probably seven or eight when I first approached Mom with the question "What's wrong with Teddy?"

"What do you mean, David? There's nothing wrong with your brother."

"I mean, he doesn't have any friends. Why's that?"

"Well, you know, David, not everyone is the same. You have lots of friends because you like people and people like you. That's wonderful! You're a sociable person. But Teddy likes to spend more time by himself, reading and working on things. That's wonderful, too. He's different from you, but everyone doesn't have to be alike. It's OK to be different."

"I know but . . . sometimes it seems he doesn't *like* people."

Mom must have sensed that I needed more than reassurance. "Sit down, David, I want to talk to you about something that happened before you were born."

Mom and I sat down side by side on the couch where she had read me stories—the Beatrix Potter series, *Wind in the Willows*, *Tom Sawyer*—and taught me about life through her explanations and commentaries. I always treasured this time with Mom for its intimacy and also for the world of imagination it opened for me. Sometimes she told me stories from her own life. But now she told me one about my brother's early life.

"When Teddy was a little baby just nine months old—before he was able to talk or understand us—he had to go to the hospital because of a rash that covered his little body. In those days, hospitals wouldn't let parents stay with a sick baby, and we were only allowed to visit him every other day for a couple of hours. I remember how your brother screamed in terror when I had to hand him over to the nurse and she took him away to another room. They had to stick lots of needles in Teddy, who was much too young to understand that everything being done to him was for his own good. He was terribly afraid, and he thought Dad and I had abandoned him to cruel strangers. He probably thought we didn't love him anymore and that we would never come back to bring him home again."

I really can't do justice to my mother's capacity for drama. Perhaps it was because of the stories and fairy tales she read to me on that old couch, but Mom had a way of entering into the emotions of the scenes she described. By the time she finished, I was deeply moved. There were tears rolling down my cheeks as I thought about the terrible suffering my brother had endured when he was a little baby.

It was an important teaching moment, and Mom took advantage of it. "David, your brother doesn't remember what happened to him, I'm sure. He was much too young. But that hospital experience hurt him deeply, and the hurt never went away completely. Please remember that you must never abandon your brother, because that's what he fears the most."

I promised Mom that I would never abandon Ted. She went on to describe her and Dad's patient efforts to help their son heal from his hospital trauma — how after they brought him home from the hospital they spoke gently and cuddled him, and tried over and over to get him to smile back at them. It took a long time, she said, before Teddy resembled the happy baby he'd been before he had to go to the hospital.

As I grew older, the story of my brother's traumatic hospital experience often came to mind as I struggled to understand Ted's quirks or to forgive his occasional insensitivity. It helped me to realize that it takes compassion to truly understand another person.

One summer a couple of years later our father, Ted Sr., caught a baby rabbit in our backyard. He placed the little animal in a wooden cage covered with a screen top. Several neighborhood kids clustered around to gape at the rabbit, and our father seemed proud to show it off. Our family, after all, had a pronounced educational bent. Dad used to teach us how to identify plants. So it was only natural that he would take pleasure in exposing the neighborhood kids to an "educational" experience — the chance to view a wild animal up close. My friends were jockeying to get a good look.

Ted was the last kid to join the onlookers, evidently curious to see what all the fuss was about. But as soon as he glimpsed the little rabbit cowering in a corner of the cage, his reaction was instinctive: "Oh, oh, let it go!" he said with panicked urgency.

Suddenly I saw everything differently. Only then did I notice that the young rabbit was trembling with fright. Only then did I realize that we were being cruel.

Dad, seeing Ted's distress, quickly carried the cage to a wooded area across the street and released the rabbit into the wild.

When I was around seven, Dad finished our attic in beautiful knotty pine so that Ted, now in high school, could have his own bedroom. The change provided us both with space and a measure of independence. But it also allowed Ted to isolate himself from the family whenever he wanted, which turned out to be rather often.

Perhaps puzzled by the long hours Ted spent quietly in his room upstairs, I remember approaching Dad with the same question I'd once asked our mother: "What's wrong with Ted?"

My father pointed out that Ted's intellectual interests set him apart from most of his classmates. While Ted read books about relativity theory, they were listening to Elvis and going to sock-hops. Someday, Dad said, Ted would go off to college and meet other young people with similar interests. He would form close friendships, would eventually marry and raise a family of his own. Ted would "find himself," Dad predicted—it just might take him a little longer.

Since Ted didn't seem to crave company, I felt privileged and rewarded whenever he'd invite me up to his room—perhaps to show me some ingenious mechanical contraption he had invented, or to let me look at his coin collection and tell me how he had acquired the more valuable coins, or to play duets he had composed using our cheap wooden recorders, or to read me a favorite story or poem. It was my brother who first introduced me to the stories and poems of Edgar Allan Poe. He once showed me a humorous drawing he'd done of Napoleon that made the emperor look quite crazed. To my preadolescent and later adolescent mind, it was wonderfully cool to have a big brother who would take me into his confidence. I treasured those times we spent together even more than I did our family vacations and excursions to the nearby forest preserve, I suppose because they were more "special." My emotional bond with Ted felt unique and very strong.

Ted left for Harvard when he was sixteen. It never would have occurred to me that my brother would suffer as a result of social isolation (and worse) there, because I had no idea he needed anything from people. I thought of him as emotionally self-sufficient, free of my "weakness" for human companionship, my need for social validation. Only years later did it occur to me that I probably mistook his introversion and strong defenses for emotional strength.

Our family photograph album holds a color picture of Ted and me standing outside our home in Evergreen Park, Illinois, sharing a grip on the handle of Ted's one bulky suitcase. Ted looks very handsome and serenely self-confident. I am the oh-so-admiring younger brother, vicariously enjoying my big brother's triumphant departure to a future without limits. My hair is combed as meticulously as Ted's. I am sporting a dressy blazer to celebrate the moment's glory and promise.

Fifty years later, as I gaze at that young boy's image, I no longer remember what it was like to be me. The picture illustrates how innocent and hopeful I was and how much I adored my older brother. The boy in the photograph was clearly a product of his family and his time. There is absolutely no shadow on that boy's faith in the world's goodness.

Perhaps that moment was the beginning of the end for Ted. He might have been ready for the academic challenges of a place like Harvard, but he was not ready developmentally or psychologically. In retrospect, our parents' one serious mistake as parents was to send him away from home at such an early age. Mastery of learning—which Ted surely had—has little to do with the mastery of life or of self. The broad reach of the rational mind doesn't extend far enough to embrace the complex challenges involved in becoming a person. But perhaps a genetic flaw, a predisposition to mental illness, would have taken Ted down eventually in any case.

What cannot be glimpsed in this picture—although it is evident in some others taken around that time—is Ted's vulnerability. His confidence in his intellect was not matched by any visceral confidence in his worth as a person, and over time the divide would only grow larger. His self-confidence became infected with doubt, recoiled, and then redoubled toward arrogance and grandiosity. His separation from loved ones, combined with his social awkwardness, fed the fear that he was unlovable. His early training sustained him for years. He knew how to maintain appearances up to a point, but it cost him great effort, and that effort eventually wore him down. What he could not sustain is an integrated ego strong enough to withstand a world constructed and inhabited by other people — a world he feared could turn or collapse on him at any moment.

Our mother, Wanda, instinctively understood her elder son's vulnerability. She trusted Harvard to keep her son safe because she deeply admired the pursuit of knowledge and tended to conflate learning and wisdom. She forgot that the eye of reason is a cool eye. She imagined Harvard as a safe haven for her brilliant son — a place where he would be appreciated by other bright people and protected from the unfriendly judgments of petty, parochial minds.

One day our parents received a letter from Harvard. Enclosed was a consent form allowing Ted to participate in a psychological research project. A parent's consent was required because Ted was still a minor, only seventeen years old, legally barred from providing consent for himself. Mom's implicit faith in the university prevented her from asking questions. Years later she recalled signing the consent form. "At the time," she said, "I was glad to give my parental consent, feeling that Teddy had some adjustment issues. I hoped these nice psychologists might help him." In doing so she unwittingly committed her son to a regimen of psychological abuse that would span the next three years of his college career.

In 1967, according to the CIA's internal assessment, hundreds of college professors on more than a hundred American college campuses were under secret contract to the CIA. So universities that wanted a piece of the action, including Harvard, decided to dispense with the ethical standard of informed consent that was embedded in the Nuremberg Code in response to Nazi atrocities. From 1953 to 1963, federal support for scientific research at Harvard increased from $8 million per year to $30 million.

One secret CIA research project that used unwitting American citizens as subjects was code-named MK Ultra. It lasted ten years and ended in 1963, shortly after Ted graduated from Harvard. MK Ultra experiments used sensory deprivation, sleep learning, subliminal projection, electronic brain stimulation, and hallucinogenic drugs to study various applications for behavior modification. One project was designed to see whether subjects could be programmed to kill on command. Experiments were conducted in penal and mental institutions and on university campuses. Some hapless human subjects went crazy, and some are known to have committed suicide.

The Harvard study my brother participated in was called "Multiform Assessments of Personality Development among Gifted College Men." It was overseen by the noted psychologist Henry Murray, who during World War II worked for the Office of Strategic Services (which later became the CIA), where he developed methodologies for interrogating prisoners of war. In his professional life, Murray was known for his brilliance and his grandiosity. In his personal life, according to his biographer, he displayed sadistic tendencies. His research on college men bears a certain resemblance to his research on prisoners of war. He was quite a big wheel in his day, perhaps as well known and influential in military and government circles as he was in academia.

Most of the records pertaining to the Murray experiments have been destroyed or lost. There is no direct evidence that the Murray experiments were funded by the CIA. However, it is clear my brother was a guinea pig in an unethical and psychologically damaging research project conducted by a team of psychological researchers who used deceptive tactics to study the effects of emotional and psychological trauma on unwitting human subjects.

Thirty-five years later, in their search for mitigating evidence that might persuade a jury to spare Ted's life, Ted's public defenders succeeded in acquiring some fragmentary records of Murray's research project. The weekly sessions in Murray's lab typically consisted of one-on-one conversations between the research subject (Ted) and a purported peer who was actually a plant: one of Murray's graduate students who had been coached to behave in an insulting way toward the subject. The idea was to upset subjects by deriding their beliefs, values, and personal characteristics.

I read a transcript of one session in which the acting research assistant focused the conversation on my brother's beard, calling it "stupid." At times during these sessions, Ted was wired up to a machine that kept track of his vital signs — and who knows what else? On occasion he would pass one of the researchers on campus and offer a shy "Hello," to which the psychologists never responded but kept on walking by, as if Ted did not exist.

We know that the experiments involved the calculated humiliation of subjects. We know that the basic premise of the research was to study how bright college students would react to aggressive, stressful attacks on their beliefs and values.

When my brother's federal public defenders asked him about the Murray experiments, he characterized his participation as "the worst experience of my life." By locating and interviewing some of the other participants, Ted's public defenders discovered that others, too, remembered the experience as highly unpleasant.

"In that case, Ted, why didn't you quit? Why did you keep going back to the lab, week after week for three years?"

"I wanted to prove that I could take it," Ted explained. "That I couldn't be broken."

TED GRADUATED FROM Harvard with a degree in mathematics. His grades were good enough to land him a teaching fellowship at another elite institution, the University of Michigan at Ann Arbor. There he published original mathematical research and won a prize for the university's best PhD thesis in mathematics that year. He was a rising star in academia. After earning his doctoral degree at Michigan, he was appointed assistant professor of mathematics at the University of California at Berkeley.

Now in high school, I tried to become my brother. I made myself into the class brain, concentrating on math, just like Ted. Although I had a few friends, all National Honor Society types, I grew more socially aloof and never dated. Once an all-star second basemen in our local Little League, I quit baseball to concentrate on academics. I took an overload of courses so I could graduate in three years. On graduation day, I was sixteen, not much older than Ted had been on his graduation day. I applied to Harvard, even, and felt very disappointed when my application was rejected. But by then I knew I was no match for my brilliant older brother. I may have been an intellectual star at Evergreen Park Community High School, but judging from the way the older faculty members swapped stories about my brother's brilliance, it was clear that Ted was one of a kind, an academic legend.

In May or June of my senior year in high school, Ted was home on vacation. One afternoon I showed him a calculus problem that I'd solved after a long, persistent struggle. Ted was impressed. "I'd guess that if I assigned the same problem to my upper-level calculus class, probably no one would be able to solve it." I was thrilled by his praise. I felt as if I had just moved into the select company of a few smart people whom Ted would naturally admire. He seemed proud of me.

A few weeks later, our family moved to a small town in Iowa where our father had been transferred by his company. This meant selling and leaving the only home I had ever really known. On moving day, Dad and I drove on ahead, while Mom and Teddy lingered behind so that Mom could give last-minute instructions to the movers. When Mom and Teddy arrived in Iowa that evening, my brother seemed uncommunicative, shut down.

Mom pulled me aside the next morning to tell me that Teddy had behaved very strangely. "David, your brother acted really oddly when the moving men were there. As I was trying to instruct them, Ted followed me everywhere around the house, saying in a loud voice, 'Make them go away! Make them go away!' It seemed so childish, and actually made it difficult for me to communicate with the moving men.

They kept looking at us with puzzled expressions, wondering why this grown man had such a problem with them. After all, they were just doing their jobs. It was embarrassing. I didn't know what to say to the men. And then on the drive here, Teddy never said a word. Four hours of silence. I tried various times to start a conversation, but he just clammed up. David, did Teddy ever tell you that he was unhappy about moving?"

"No," I said. "He didn't." In the back of my mind, I wondered if Ted was upset to see his house of memories dismantled, perhaps signifying the loss of the only safe emotional refuge he'd ever known. Didn't he know that all things change? And that the loss of our material house (as poignant as that might feel) in no way endangered the sense of home Mom and Dad had always maintained for us?

OVER THE NEXT TEN YEARS, Ted and I came to relate more as adult peers than as big and little brother. I came to enjoy a feeling of greater equality with my brother and was pleased to see that he acknowledged and for the most part encouraged my independence. But I also felt myself gradually drifting away from him. One summer when I was home from college and Ted was back from California, we spent a month camping together on Michigan's Upper Peninsula. The following year, 1969, he abruptly quit his professor's job at the University of California at Berkeley, and that summer we traveled across western Canada looking for a piece of land for him to homestead.

Ted had written our parents a letter announcing that he had come to the conclusion, after much thought, that technological development was threatening to humanity and to the environment. His overriding concern was the erosion of human freedom and autonomy brought on by technology. (Recently he had absorbed Jacques Ellul's *Technological Society*, a wide-ranging critique of technology.) Since much of technology was based on mathematics, Ted explained, he'd decided to give up his career in mathematics. In fact, he had grown so concerned about technology that he was determined to remove himself personally from it as far as he could. To this end, he would attempt to live in the wilderness (or what was left of it) as primitive peoples had done for most of human history.

I was amazed, actually in awe of my brother's brave and principled gesture. Few people have the courage to make significant sacrifices based on well-considered principles. And how many people get to do what they want in life, instead of following a path prescribed by others? I was inspired by my big brother's courage in abandoning the more conventional path.

Ted expected our parents to be angry about his decision to quit his career. On the contrary, they were cautiously supportive. After Ted and I left home, they respected our personal decisions. Privately, though, Mom expressed concern: "Dave," she confided, "I don't think Teddy's decision really has much to do with technology. I'm worried that he doesn't know how to accept other people or be accepted by them. I'm afraid he's running away from a society he doesn't know how to relate to." Yet for a time she indulged a fond hope that Ted would get the dream of living a primitive life out of his system and return to teaching.

In 1971—after an unsuccessful attempt to get a Canadian home-stead permit and a brief stint living with our parents—Ted followed me to Montana, where I had migrated after college.

I'd been living in Great Falls, Montana, for about a year—working a blue-collar job at a zinc smelter, fashioning my own anticareerist, populist narrative—when one afternoon my landlord knocked on my door and told me that my father was on the phone urgently requesting to speak with me. Since I didn't have a phone, my family usually com-municated with me by mail. In some alarm, I followed my landlord back to his apartment, expecting bad news.

"Dave, have you seen Ted?" Dad asked. He sounded worried.

"I thought he was with you."

"He was, until the day before yesterday. He must have left before dawn. He didn't tell us where he was going. We were hoping he was with you."

"No, I haven't seen him, but it's a long drive from Chicago to Montana. Didn't he leave you a note or anything?"

"Yes, Dave, but he didn't say where he was going."

"That's kind of strange."

"He left us a goodbye note." Pause. "He said he was sorry if he'd failed us. He said we shouldn't have any regrets because we were good parents. Dave, I have this uneasy feeling that your brother left in a very bad state of mind. His goodbye sounded so final—almost like a suicide note."

I asked Dad to read me Ted's letter. After hearing it, I thought it could be interpreted in different ways. Dad seemed to be jumping to conclusions—something he seldom did—so I did my best to calm his anxiety. I registered some surprise: worry was more in Mom's department than Dad's. I promised to let my parents know the moment I saw or heard from Ted.

Early the next morning, a loud knocking on my door woke me up, and I was relieved to find Ted standing there. He looked OK.

"I have a proposal for you," he said abruptly.

"I thought you were with Mom and Dad."

"I just couldn't stay there anymore," he said flatly.

Ted then suggested that we pool our resources to a buy a parcel of land to live on. I was pleased that Ted was OK, that he had a plan for the future, and that his plan included me. The land turned out to be the 1.4-acre plot six miles outside Lincoln where he built his now iconic ten-by-twelve cabin and he lived a seemingly inoffensive hermit's life for the next twenty-five years. I stayed in Great Falls working at the smelter, thinking that eventually I might build a cabin next to Ted's.

MORE AND MORE, Ted's intellectual interests shifted from mathematics to anthropology. He especially enjoyed reading about "primitive" tribes. Once, invoking his vision of an ideal society, he described to me hunter-gatherer communities based on reciprocity and trust— "You know . . . like our family." If someone had told me that in another five years Ted would be writing letters of bitter recrimination to our parents, I would have been surprised, if not shocked. As late as the late 1970s, he invited me to join him in a quest for remote land in the Canadian wilderness where we could live together far from the bane of civilization. By then, however, it was clear to me that I would be quite unhappy to let my life shrink to one relationship with my civilization-hating brother.

On my next visit home, Mom handed me a book—*This Stranger, My Son*, by Louise Wilson—and asked me to read it. Wilson's book describes the journey of a mother seeking to understand and obtain help for her mentally ill son. She describes in painful detail her son's distorted perceptions of the world; the psychiatrists' inclination to blame the parents (particularly the mother); her own sense of guilt and shame; the unavailability of effective help; never knowing precisely where her son's authentic self ended and where his intractable mental illness took over; her endless worry over her son's problems and uncertain future; and, above all, the disintegration of her son's peace and happiness.

When I finished reading the book, I handed it back to Mom and asked, "Mom, did you ask me to read this book because it reminded you of Ted?"

She was quiet for a moment. Then she said, "Well, parts of it really *did* make me think of your brother. Did you have the same feeling?" I could see the searching concern in her eyes.

"Yes, well, there are some resemblances."

"Not that I think Ted is schizophrenic," she hastened to add, "but maybe he has tendencies in that direction."

ON ONE HAND, a change in how I saw my brother was inevitable. Most adoring younger brothers take their older brothers off their pedestal at some point. Idols show their clay feet eventually. In a healthy relationship, disillusioned hero-worship is replaced by mature affection—and Ted certainly had a lot of likable qualities. He was still smart, independent, and principled. There was also, by this time, a kind of despondency in him that I found very poignant. He didn't seem to want any of the things most people crave: being loved and admired; having money, comfort, or worldly success. In his humility and integrity, he resembled the saints of old—except that his asceticism was completely disconnected from faith, love, or hope. On the contrary, it seemed haunted by defeatism. I also sensed that he expected me to live the same way and to share his deeply pessimistic views.

When I left Montana to take a job teaching high school English in the Midwest in 1973, my mother asked a typically worried question: "Did you say goodbye to Ted before you left?"

Her question caught me up short, and I answered a little defensively: "Well, he knew I was going." I would have had to drive 180 miles round-trip to see Ted, I told her. In the back of my mind, I was thinking that I couldn't spend the rest of my life shackled to my brother. He never said he needed me anyway. Mom was expecting too much, I thought. But I also remembered my early promise never to abandon my brother. Did it feel to him, on some level, that I was abandoning him now?

Ted's angry—well, blistering—letters to our parents started arriving in the mid-1970s. The gist was that he had been unhappy all his life because Mom and Dad had never truly loved him. They pushed him academically to feed their own egos. They never taught him appropriate social skills because they didn't care about his happiness. These letters were not an invitation to talk, but an indictment filled with highly dramatized and—in my view—distorted memories. Yet in Ted's own mind, his conclusion was as rock solid as a mathematical proof.

At first I thought he had simply lost his temper. After all, he was emotionally intense and spent nearly all his time alone. He'd given up a promising but unfulfilling academic career to live in the woods — and still he wasn't happy. So it was not surprising that he could sometimes lose his grip and say things he didn't really mean. It could happen to almost anyone.

But when I wrote to Ted, hoping I could help him understand the pain his letter had caused our parents and apologize to them, I received a series of increasingly disturbed replies that convinced me he hadn't just lost his temper: every recrimination he'd flung at Mom and Dad was based in a fixed belief system. I was surely Ted's closest human contact, yet I'd never seen any of this coming. And now nothing I said could even begin to shake Ted's judgment of Mom and Dad. At one point he warned me that if I continued defending Mom and Dad, he'd cut me out of his life as well. Once he did so, he said, it would be forever. For the next ten years, more or less, I thought there was a chance I could persuade Ted to see things differently.

A few occasional crises during this period made me think my brother might be seriously disturbed. In the late '70s, for instance, he returned to Illinois to earn some money. For a time our family was reunited, living in a house that Mom and Dad had bought after Dad's company transferred him back to Chicago.

Teddy and I worked briefly at the same factory, until he started harassing a female coworker and I had to intercede. At first my brother appeared to be in love (which I noted with pleasant amazement, since my brother had never dated or even talked much about women). He took the girl out for dinner at nice restaurants and for walks in the forest preserve. But he was utterly devastated when she politely broke off their relationship, saying she only wanted to be friends. The next day Ted began anonymously posting offensive limericks about the woman around the workplace. I found his behavior intolerable: she was a nice person who didn't deserve such humiliating treatment. Angry, I confronted Ted and told him that he had to stop or I'd find a way to make him stop. So the next day when Ted posted another of the nasty limericks, I went to the plant's supervisor and had my brother dismissed. Ted needed to know he had no right to treat people badly — as he had treated our parents, as he was now treating this poor woman. Only after my anger cooled did it sink in how much my brother must have craved an intimate relationship and how unequal he was to the challenges of being in one.

Ted locked himself in his room at Mom and Dad's for three days. During that time I wondered if and when we should summon a crisis response team. Mom was a basket case; Dad was withdrawn, indecisive. I imagined that Ted would never be the same after this incident and that our relationship would never recover from his bad behavior and my disloyalty.

After three days, however, Ted emerged from his room and abruptly asked me to read a long letter he had written, on condition that I never speak with him about it. The letter was more explanation than apology; its apologetic elements were tainted with self-justification. Essentially, what he wanted to communicate was that he had been deeply and desperately lonely for a very long time.

With Ted's half-apology and my keeping my promise not to discuss the matter our relationship seemed to recover, more or less. But looking back now, I can see there was a downward spiral. As time went on, there were more and more topics we had to avoid because discussing them upset Ted. There was an undertone of stress in the letters we regularly exchanged. For me that stress stemmed from my brother's harsh treatment of our parents. Ted wanted me to agree with him about everything; I wanted to defend my own ego as an independent person, but most of all I wanted to defend Mom and Dad against Ted's cruel opinion of them. They were kind and generous to him even when he broke their hearts. I felt increasingly concerned as I began to realize that I was not going to change my brother's mind.

The Irish poet W. B. Yeats once said that responsibility begins with the power to imagine. I suppose he meant that only after we imagine ourselves in another person's shoes, experiencing what they suffer, do we see beyond our own self-interest and take responsibility for others' welfare. I'd often thought there was something a little peculiar, even paradoxical, about Ted's attitude toward the imagination. Generally speaking he tended to dismiss, repress, and denigrate the imagination. Seemingly pragmatic, he viewed the imagination as a manifestation of psychological weakness, a compensation for life's insufficiency. At best, it was an empty entertainment; at worst, a vehicle of escape from reality into fantasy.

On the other hand, Ted could experience sharp, poignant sympathy for people he regarded as vulnerable—particularly children or those living on the margins of society. He could experience and occasionally expressed deep compassion for those who were powerless and suffering. However, he could never imagine anyone in a relatively powerful position as suffering—or at least not undeservedly.

On rare occasions, Ted endowed his imagination with a power that was visionary and even revelatory. In one dramatic letter, he told me that he was about to "draw aside the veil" on his soul for the first and last time. Then he described a dream of exceptional emotional intensity. It focused on a sinister, satanic character who continually changed shape, impersonated or became identical with some of my closest friends (including Linda); this demon attempted to lure me away to some lost, hellish place from which there could be no return. Filled with desperation, Ted had to kill the satanic figure in order to save me.

On one hand, Ted was telling me that he loved me. On the other hand, he seemed to be telling me that he hated and feared my closest friends. I half wondered if what Ted described to me was a dream at all.

MY MARRIAGE TO LINDA was the proverbial last straw as far as Ted was concerned. Maybe he understood—whether consciously or not — the implications of bringing another fresh, intelligent mind into the family. Perhaps it forced him to see his little brother differently. After receiving the news that I'd left the desert to live with Linda, he wrote me a nasty letter berating me for making what he called "the biggest mistake" of my life. He'd somehow decided that Linda, whom he'd never met, was a terrible person. At the end of the letter, he disowned me as his brother.

I found myself suddenly caught between anger at Ted's arrogance, and deep concern that my brother was prepared to sever his last emotional tie. Didn't he understand that love is unlimited? — that my love for Linda didn't decrease my love for him? Once again I recalled how years earlier Mom had cautioned me that Ted's worst fear was a fear of abandonment.

Two years later, it was Linda who made me confront the growing evidence that my brother was suffering from a mental disorder. "But that's the way he thinks!" I protested at first. I remember her then pointing to a bizarre passage in a letter I'd just received from Ted. "David, read this. People who are healthy in their minds don't think like this."

In the letter, Ted had written: "I have got to know, I have GOT TO, GOT TO, GOT TO know that every last tie joining me to this stinking family has been cut FOREVER and that I will never NEVER have to communicate with any of you again. . . . I've got to do it NOW. I can't tell you how desperate I am. . . . It is killing me."

Linda persuaded me to discuss Ted's letters with a psychiatrist. I made an appointment and sent him two or three of Ted's letters ahead of time. The psychiatrist's prognosis was not encouraging: "David, these letters show symptoms of serious mental illness. I'm not going to make a diagnosis based on a couple of letters, because that's not how we make a diagnosis. But I will say that I think your brother needs treatment, and I don't mean just talk therapy. Talking alone probably won't help him without some chemical intervention as well."

"I'm sure Ted would never agree to treatment, especially not with chemicals," I said glumly. "He'd be afraid of being poisoned, of having his sharp intellect dulled. He might see it as society's plot to control him."

"I can well imagine that," the psychiatrist said. "Again, I'm not making a diagnosis here, but in these letters I see features consistent with schizophrenia. There's some highly paranoid ideation. Extreme defensiveness. Probably your brother would never voluntarily agree to treatment."

"Are you suggesting, then, that we pursue *in*voluntary treatment?"

The doctor pondered this idea for a moment. "I don't think I'd recommend that, either. You really are stuck between a rock and a hard place. Without treatment, your brother's illness will probably get worse. But if you pursue involuntary commitment, you may lose any chance of having a relationship with him. You probably wouldn't get him committed anyway, because you'd have to go to court and prove he represents an imminent danger to himself or others."

"I've always had a fear that Ted might someday hurt himself."

"But your fear alone doesn't constitute evidence that would convince a judge," the doctor concluded.

Linda joined me at my next appointment with the psychiatrist a few days later. We needed to strategize—put our heads together and figure out how to help Ted. But it seemed as if we were only clutching at straws, since Ted had made himself so unreachable.

As we were about to leave the psychiatrist's office, Linda asked abruptly, "Do you think he might become violent?"

The doctor paused. When he spoke he seemed to choose his words carefully: "The underlying theme of schizophrenia is *fear*. When a person experiences intense fear, especially if they feel trapped and cornered, then violence against oneself or other people is never out of the realm of possibility."

Much later, while reading Ted's diary at the behest of his legal defense team, I stumbled upon a piece of information that astonished me. It turns out that a couple years before Linda and I tried unsuccessfully to connect Ted with treatment, he'd independently written to the county mental health service in Helena, sixty miles from his cabin, requesting therapy by mail. Ted didn't know that he had a delusional disorder like schizophrenia, but he knew that he suffered from insomnia and high anxiety. Somewhat naively, he hoped to receive professional help in the form of answers to his questions via the U.S. mail.

My brother was informed by return post that the system didn't work that way. He was told that he would have to appear in person and find a way to pay for services—both insurmountable barriers from Ted's point of view.

FIVE YEARS LATER, my feelings toward Ted shifted after I read his manifesto in the *Washington Post* and began coming to grips with the horrific possibility that Ted might be the long-sought serial bomber. Again, it was Linda who pried open my mind, Linda who urged me to read the manifesto. I had never considered Ted capable of violence. In fact, my only fear along those lines was the haunting worry that he might someday kill himself.

Suddenly it felt as if my brother and I were central characters in a grandiose tragedy. I began to discern a frightening symmetry in our lives that led me to the terrible dilemma that Linda and I then faced: do nothing and run the risk that Ted might kill again, or turn him in and accept the likelihood that he would be executed for his crimes.

I could not reconcile the conflict between our moral obligation and my love for my brother, could not make a decision without sacrificing one for the other. But perhaps, I thought, we would wake up some day and see our situation differently. Perhaps our sacrifice—compelled by reason and necessity—would feel less painful now that I had come closer to acknowledging the worst about my brother. If we waited for some magical resolution of our dilemma, we could end up waiting forever. We could end up waiting until someone else was blown up.

The alternatives looked too stark to be true, more like literature than life. Looking back over our lives as brothers, I began to see how every step led us to this terrible juncture. Now I felt trapped inside the narrative of our lives, my identity forever defined by the fate of being Ted Kaczynski's brother. I wanted out of that role. I wanted to make my own choices in life, not have them foisted upon me. I wanted to create my own story. And yet to choose to do nothing was itself a choice. There was no escape. I was boxed in by the awful dilemma, and for some time I felt engulfed in a vision of the universe as dark as Ted's.

When federal agents entered my brother's tiny cabin near Lincoln, Montana, on April 3, 1996, they discovered bomb-making parts and plans, a carbon copy of the Unabomber's manifesto, and—most chilling of all—another live bomb found under his bed, wrapped and apparently ready to be mailed to someone.

My resentment of Ted strangely melted away. The way I was accustomed to thinking about him, my usual frame of reference, no longer worked. Now there was just emptiness and deep pity in my heart where my brother had been.

I wondered how Ted would receive the news that I'd turned him in. I hoped he might understand on some level why I had done so and not hate me for it. How would it feel to my paranoid brother to be turned in by the one person he had loved and trusted? I thought it must feel like the confirmation of his darkest thought. Mom's warning voice from childhood echoed in my ears: *David, you must never abandon your brother, because that's what he fears the most.*

I recalled a letter I had received from Ted in 1988, one year before I moved in with Linda. At the top of the page was taped a small picture cut out from the newspaper of a young boy in a baseball cap grinning happily. Beneath the picture, Ted wrote a message that was uncharacteristically sentimental. "Dear Dave, This picture reminds me of you when you were young. You were always such a cheerful, happy kid. I, on the other hand, have never been happy. I've never even had a close friend. I want you to know, in case anything happens to me, that you are the one person that I've ever loved."

In case anything happens to me sounded a bit foreboding, but I'd assumed he meant some sort of accident, probably during one of his long backpacking trips into the rugged Montana wilderness.

I was touched by this letter, although it gave me a slightly uneasy feeling as well. Like other affectionate letters I'd received from Ted, it seemed to float up out of a deep and inescapable well of loneliness.

Some months after meeting with Ted's original lawyer, I heard a story about Ted's reaction when he first learned that I'd turned him in. Since the story came to me thirdhand, I can't vouch for its veracity, but it sounded plausible enough.

"Did you know it was your brother who turned you in?" the lawyer asked.

"That's impossible," Ted reportedly said. "David loves me. He'd never do that."

Some days later, persuaded otherwise, Ted told his attorneys that he had resolved once and for all, regardless of circumstances, not to communicate with his family ever again. To date, he has kept that pledge.

IT HAS OCCURRED TO me that Ted and I are almost like disowned parts of each other. Ted the Unabomber represents the violence and pessimism that I reject. David the putative "moral hero" represents the inauthenticity of hope in a world gone fundamentally awry. Ted's cruelty stigmatizes my good name; but my reputation for goodness comes at his expense. Like all contrived opposites, we reinforce one another. The worst thing he can do to me is to deny any opportunity for reconciliation. Hope of reconciliation is something I am bound to maintain, but it costs me little — only the sneaking sense that some part of me is missing.

As a young kid I had lots of boyhood pals, almost like temporary brothers my own age who would come and go in my life. Unlike my real brother, they turned out to be replaceable. Many of my post–high school friendships, however, endured much longer. I spent four years with the same college roommate, and we've grown even closer over the years. If something ever happened to Joel, I would grieve as much as I would for Ted. Our conversations pick up just where they leave off, even after a gap of years. I discover in my friend much of the openness and reciprocity that I never found in Ted. He was there for me in my worst hour. There is a level of trust and respect between us that makes the whole world seem stable and sane at its core, simply because this kind of relationship is possible. I suppose it's what Martin Buber named the "I-Thou"—a recognition of the relational structure of our human reality.

Several months after Ted's arrest, I made contact with one of my brother's surviving victims—Gary Wright of Salt Lake City, Utah. In one sense, he represented someone whose experience of the Unabomber saga was the polar opposite of mine. Part of me desperately needed to open a door to that "other side," the victims' side. Ted would not talk to me, and, not surprisingly, neither would most of his victims or their family members. A lot of worlds got shattered by Ted's bombs. Probably it was foolish of me—even self-indulgent—to imagine that I could reassemble any of those pieces in the hope of making my world whole again. But with incredible grace, Gary volunteered to help me. In the years since our first awkward phone conversation, we too have become as close and indispensable to one another as brothers.

On the evening of September 11, 2001, I was home alone in Schenectady. Linda was away in Illinois caring for her sick parents. We were terribly worried about Linda's brother and his wife, whose apartment in Lower Manhattan was not far from the World Trade Center site; and also about our niece attending college in Philadelphia, cut off from news of her parents because of the telephone outage. I suppose being the brother of a so-called terrorist made the events of that day more disturbing, if possible, than they otherwise would have been for me. I learned from Linda that our sister-in-law in Manhattan had been on the phone with Linda's mother when she saw the second tower fall. Then the phone line was cut off. I managed to reach my niece at her dorm room and found her as sane and sensible as always, somehow managing to give back more reassurance than she took. I couldn't bear to watch the news. But the silence felt equally unbearable. I wondered what my brother might be thinking about all of this.

The phone rang again. "Hey, Dave, it's good to hear your voice! I know you take a lot of trips to New York City. I'm so glad to know that you're OK." It was Gary Wright.

On a night when just about everyone in America was checking in with their closest family and friends, Gary Wright made a call to the brother of the man who'd tried to kill him. It was reassuring to know that I lived in a world where such a call was possible. In that moment, I knew Gary would be my friend for life.

Gary and I are virtual blood brothers. Our bond forged through violence is as powerful and deep as any other. We also share a base of values. Our bond is as much a bond of choice as one of happenstance. Tragedy has given us both an unexpected gift. My life is infinitely richer because of Gary's friendship. Nothing can compensate me for losing Ted, but I find a poetic balance in having gained a new brother in Gary. Our choices end up reshaping the universe — at least the universe we know.

No one lives a life without loss. Loss of loved ones. Loss of innocence. Loss of dreams and hopes. Loss of each precious moment as quickly as it passes. Loss of our own lives in the end.

SOMETIMES WHEN I'M driving down the road, I'll glance in the mirror and for a split second I'll see Ted driving the car behind me. A moment later, I realize it's just another guy with a beard. A guy with a completely different mind and a life all his own. Anyone could be my brother, I realize, if fate had just arranged things a little differently. No matter — a flood of memories rushes in. So many memories: some sad, some anxious, some happy and loving, but all of them poignant. What happened to those two little boys who grew up together in a different, more hopeful world in 1950s America? Or to the two young men who spent an entire summer camping together in western Canada in 1969? Back then, I never could have imagined my life without Ted.

As we were driving back from Canada to Illinois in August 1969, I was feeling eager to return home, thinking about regular baths, Mom's home cooking, an opportunity to catch up on the world's news, perhaps even a chance to see Linda before she returned to school. I wanted to rejoin the stream of my life after this memorable detour. Ted and I were camped out in a county park in the grasslands of Nebraska, lying on our backs side by side, gazing up at the immense, starry sky as warm summer breezes stirred the tall grass around us.

"I wish we were home," I said.

"Really? I wish we didn't have to go back," Ted said.

It was a defining difference. But now I too wish we could relive that moment.

<CHAPTER 2 >

LIFE FORCE

IN HER LAST DAYS, THE ACUITY of her pain and sharp intelligence blunted by morphine, my mother would wake up often at night and share words and phrases that were rich with emotional significance for her.

When the process of dying is prolonged, the final days and weeks may involve an inward turning reckoning with life, a final struggle with its conflicts, its unresolved problems and unanswered questions.

Mother's speech was slow and labored, yet her desire to match the words with their intended meaning was as strong as ever. And there was something new: a mantralike quality, a music of repetition, a need to either make sure she was understood or to score the meaning deeply.

"Beautiful . . . golden colors . . ."
"Memories . . . memories . . . memories."
"I saw a ghost . . . a ghost of the world."

Once she said she dreamed she had fallen into a deep hole. There were periods of agitation when she found her circumstances — the pain, the discomfort and restlessness going on without visible end — to be unendurable.

"I want to die! I want to die!" she said over and over again. With immense effort, she would pull her tiny torso to a sitting position and, by grasping the protective bedrail, laboriously swing her legs over the side of the bed. She wanted to go somewhere, but there was nowhere to go. Over time I learned that the best way to calm and protect her was to sit beside her on the bed and clasp my arm around her shoulder for comfort and support. She would then sigh deeply and rest her head against my shoulder — her big head atop her scrawny body, no larger than a child's.

Attempting to comfort her on her unfathomable journey made me feel like a parent for the first time.

Mom had a rational mind that guided her understanding but left her at somewhat of a loss to grapple with life's ambiguities. So I imagine her drawn-out final accounting of her life as she withdrew inward over several days and nights was a frustrating experience.

But her spirit lightened near the end.

I'd slept on the floor beside her bed for several nights in case she needed something.

"David!" I heard her call in the middle of her last lucid night.

"Yes, Mom?" I rose to my knees at her bedside. "What is it?"

"Did you fart?"

"What?" (I thought I might have misheard her.)

"Did you fart?"

"Yes," I said sheepishly. "I didn't think you'd notice."

"We should call you 'Boomer'!"

Then she launched into one of her interminable mantras, repeating my new name *Boomer* again and again, lengthening the vowel sound: *Boooomer.* Suddenly, as if taking full measure of our situation, she exclaimed, "Oh, sweetheart!" and hugged my head tightly to her chest, repeating *Sweetheart* several times until it, too, morphed into a more amusing, sly endearment, *Sweetfart*!

MOM GREW UP IN A Polish-Catholic immigrant family in southern Ohio in the 1920s. The family was poor and dysfunctional. Her mother was alcoholic, occasionally violent, and quite possibly mentally ill. Her father slaved away at a steel mill in the pre-union era, working six and a half days a week to support his family.

In Mom's fondest memories of her father, he read Polish folk tales aloud to the family. Because of his mild temperament, he'd been cast as Jesus in miracle plays in his home village in rural Poland. But that same softness of temper prevented him from standing up to his unstable wife, even when it became necessary to protect the children during her drunken rages. So Mom grew up shielding her younger siblings, which made her the target of her mother's anger.

Immigrants, especially Poles, were unwelcome at that time and place. Once the Ku Klux Klan burned a cross on a hill above the family's home—a home her father had bought in the better part of town, where Poles were not supposed to be.

Mom attended a one-room rural schoolhouse that became her refuge from the chaos of her home life and the xenophobia of her neighbors. Her teacher, a young woman who probably had no college education, evidently had a gift for connecting emotionally with her students. After school, she would walk partway home with a group of them, and on one such occasion a child piped up, "Wanda reads good, don't she?"

As Mom tells it, the teacher replied, "Oh yes, Wanda is a *very* good reader," and placed her arm fondly around Mom's shoulders.

This may have been the first time my mother had been praised and treated with affection. Eighty years later, as she recounted this story to a young woman she'd befriended, tears starting flowing down Mom's cheeks.

Positive attention from a teacher proved to be a pivotal moment in Mom's development: learning was her gift and her personal validation. Books would become her source of hope for the future and her escape from the squalor and chaos of her surroundings. As she grew older, she greatly admired the novels by Charles Dickens that exposed the social inequities of the industrial revolution. But that kindly young teacher, I suspect, was the original inspiration behind Mom's intellectual growth and her capacity to dream—perhaps even the main reason little Wanda was able to survive her difficult childhood with a sense of self-worth and purpose.

When she married at age twenty-two, her mission in life turned to raising children. Two ideals shone clearly in her mind: her children would be well educated so they could benefit humanity, and they would be protected from the abuses she herself had endured in childhood.

She intended to make sure that ignorance, bigotry, and hatred would never touch us.

I ATTACH IMPORTANCE TO my early memories and assume they must have survived in order to tell me something about my own mind. In one of these memories, I am ensconced on a couch alongside my mother, who is reading me a story whose name I don't recall. I am about five or six years old. We have come upon a word—*empathy*—that is new to me. I've heard about sympathy, but not empathy. I've been taught that it is good to feel sympathy for people in pain, and I know from my own experience that I can feel this emotion under certain circumstances. Now Mom is trying to connect a nuance of language to a nuance of emotional experience.

"David, sympathy is like feeling sorry *for* someone in pain, but empathy is like feeling sorry *with* someone. Empathy happens when you are able to imagine yourself in another person's place. Even if you don't share the other person's pain at that moment, you might remember having experienced that pain before; or even if you've never experienced the same pain, you might remember a similar kind of pain that you yourself have experienced; or even if you've never experienced a pain that's anything like it, you might still be able to imagine what it's like by putting yourself in the other person's place, asking yourself, 'How would it feel?' That's empathy. Sympathy might go away after a moment, for example if you turn away and decide to stop seeing another person's pain. But empathy is something that stays with you a long time. It's something that can make you into a good person — what we call a *humanitarian*."

I CAN'T IMAGINE MOM'S pain when she experienced the first full blast of her elder son's rejection. It arrived in the form of a twenty-three-page letter, around 1977, that accused her and Dad of being emotionally abusive parents. His hand seemingly shaking with rage as he wrote, Ted grew increasingly upset as he wove details from his childhood into an immense, dark tapestry of rejection and humiliation. In one place he noted that Mom once yelled at him for throwing his dirty socks under the bed. She should have known, Ted fumed, that tossing dirty socks under a bed was more or less normal behavior for an adolescent boy. (But shouldn't Ted have realized that yelling about a pile of dirty socks under the bed was more or less normal behavior for an adolescent boy's mother?)

Some of his complaints were more serious. For instance, he said Mom and Dad pressed him to attend Harvard instead of Oberlin College, which was more intimate, closer to home, and more supportive of his musical interests. To Ted, this meant Mom and Dad were more concerned with status and prestige than with his happiness. In retrospect, Harvard was not the best choice for Ted. But choices are rarely so clear without hindsight. And what parents of humble background wouldn't urge their talented child to reach for the stars? Their college preference surely did not mean, as Ted insisted, that they were selfish, uncaring, abusive parents.

Mom and Dad were terribly upset when they showed me Ted's letter, hoping that I could help them understand it.

"David, what did we do wrong? Were we really such terrible parents?" As a family, we revisited the letter again and again. It hurt me to see our parents' happiness poisoned as they struggled to defend themselves against the letter's harsh tone while maintaining loving feelings toward their troubled son. A child's unhappiness is inevitably a parent's deep regret.

Until then Mom had been wont to say, "You know, I think Ted is maturing" (kind of an odd thing to say about a man in his midthirties). But now that fond hope was unveiled as wishful thinking. The letter ran the developmental spectrum, suggesting a three-year-old's tantrum translated into an adult's analytical language. What I found most disturbing was that the message seemed calculated to inflict pain.

It's not uncommon for unhappy people to take it out on others. When things go wrong, we typically look for someone to blame, and at those times we often say things we regret. But as much as I tried to normalize Ted's behavior, a voice in the back of my mind told me that Ted had ventured down a one-way path. Something had shifted dramatically in his world — a world so much stranger and darker than I had previously guessed. No, Ted was not growing up.

In years to follow, there were more long, angry letters and even longer silences. Mom's hand-wringing and soul-searching never stopped. She seemed resigned to a perpetual state of anguish and worry, whereas Dad's resignation took a different form: "He knows what he's doing," he said once.

Every time I visited home, Mom would ask, "Have you heard from Ted? Is he OK?" I was Mom's only contact with her firstborn son. Our family discussions assumed a repetitive, slightly obsessive quality as we searched for answers beyond our reach. Had she and Dad pushed Ted too hard academically? I didn't think so, because Teddy preferred reading and studying to playing with other kids. Had they neglected his emotional social needs? I remember Mom inviting other kids over to the house only to see my brother give them the cold shoulder. Were we witnessing the long-term effects of a childhood abandonment trauma (i.e., his storied "hospital experience")? To me that explanation made the most sense. If separation was what my brother unconsciously feared, then perhaps he was preempting the inevitable by rejecting his family. But when we came down to it, we could find no reliable way of rationalizing the mysterious processes inside my brother's mind.

Unfortunately, Mom's worst nightmare about what could be wrong with Ted didn't come remotely close to the truth.

ONE TERRIBLE DAY IN March 1996, I climbed the stairs to Mom's new second-floor apartment in the village of Scotia, just across the Mohawk River from Schenectady, New York.

Linda and I decided that it would be best for me to face Mom on my own. Linda had been the first to suspect Ted. She was also the driving force behind our investigation of Ted and of the anguished process of ethical decision-making that soon consumed us. We didn't want Mom displacing any possible resentment onto her daughter-in-law.

When Mom opened her door, I saw stacks of cardboard boxes that she hadn't had time to empty since her move from Illinois. Quickly, Mom's smile turned to a look of dismay.

"David, you look terrible! Is something wrong? Tell me, what *is* it?"

"Mom, I think you'd better sit down."

Perhaps it was the years of nagging worry, or else it was a mother's radarlike intuition, but Mom immediately homed in on her elder son: "Is it Ted? Oh, my God! Did something happen to Ted?" I could hear the panic rising in her voice. "Oh, David, tell me, please!"

"Mom, as far as I know, Ted's in good health. But I do have something troubling to discuss with you. Sit down, Mom, please."

Mom's La-Z-Boy chair had survived the purges of her move and was now in the corner of her apartment, near the window. When I picture Mom now, I often see her sitting in that chair, reading, watching television, or chatting with a visitor on the nearby couch.

I was much too agitated to sit down. I paced the floor back and forth, searching for some painless way to deliver my awful news.

"Mom, have you ever read any newspaper articles about the Unabomber?"

I saw her tense up, although as it turned out Mom had little more than a passing knowledge of the Unabomber's activities. She read the newspaper and watched a fair amount of television, but crime stories held little interest for her. I gave her a quick summary of the Unabomber's course of bombings and terror. I talked about the places the Unabomber had been. Then I reminded her that Ted had frequented some of the same places. I told her about the publication of the Unabomber's manifesto, with its broad critique of technology.

"Mom, you know about Ted's obsession with technology."

As I continued to outline comparisons, I saw Mom gazing at me with a strange look on her face. Although I could read horror in her expression, her other emotions were unclear to me. Did she think I'd lost my mind? Was she horrified at the possibility that Ted might be a murderer? Or was she more horrified, perhaps, that I could even think of my brother as a murderer?

On the end table next to Mom's chair stood her favorite photograph of Teddy and me, a picture taken in our living room by a professional photographer when I was about three years old and Teddy about ten. Perched on my brother's shoulder was his pet parakeet. Teddy displayed much of the shyness but none of the rigidity evident in later photographs. Instead there was a softness, a vulnerability in his expression as he made himself a perch for the nervous little creature. My eyes glittered with pride, happy to be pictured with my big brother, pleased to be included at the center of attention.

I never questioned that Mom loved both Ted and me with all her heart. But would she still love me when I told her what I had done?

By now I was crying a little, wiping away tears and talking a bit faster. I decided I'd better come clean: "Mom, I'm really concerned that Ted might be involved in these bombings. I'm really scared."

"Oh. Don't tell anyone!" she blurted out.

It was the last thing I wanted to hear. But her reaction was understandable, even predictable, given a mother's instinct to protect her child. For years, she had been consumed with worry over her elder son's vulnerability. He was so different, so seemingly out of his element in a world of social conventions that most of us take for granted.

"Mom, I've already told someone," I said flatly. "I've approached the FBI and shared my suspicions with them. Now they're investigating Ted to see if he might be the Unabomber."

Life is full of tests, I suppose—tests big and small. Sometimes we see them coming, as Linda and I did, and sometimes they're sprung on us without warning, as happened to Mom that day. We can only hope we're prepared when the test comes.

Linda and I had had the luxury of time. We also had each other. Mom, on the other hand, had no time to think things through, nor anyone she could use as a sounding board.

After a stunned pause, she silently got up from her chair and came up to me. She was a very small woman—under five feet tall—whereas I'm over six feet. She reached up, put her arms around my neck, and gently pulled me down to plant a kiss on my cheek.

The first thing she said was "David, I can't imagine what you've been going through." It is still extraordinary to me that in this moment—probably the worst moment of her life—Mom's first concern was for my feelings, not her own.

Then she said the most comforting thing imaginable: "David, I know you love Ted. I know you wouldn't have done this unless you felt you had to."

With those words, I understood that she owned me as her son. I hadn't lost her love. I realized now that the three of us—Mom, Linda, and I—would face this ordeal together.

Still, she was where I'd been six months earlier when Linda first approached me with her suspicions. She couldn't imagine that Ted could actually hurt someone.

"You know, Dave," she said, "Ted has never been violent. He loves children and animals. We've always known there's a deeply sensitive side to Ted—maybe too sensitive. I can't imagine that he would wantonly attack and hurt people. I can't believe he's capable of anything like that. Maybe it's a good thing you've gone to the FBI. They're going to investigate and find out that he's completely innocent. You'll see. This whole thing will go away like a bad dream."

"I'm glad you feel that way, Mom," I said with resignation, "but there's something else I need to tell you. There are some people from the FBI who would like very much to talk to you. Would you be willing to talk with them?"

That set her off balance. "Well, I really don't know anything. What could they possibly want to talk to me about? I don't know anything about this."

I explained to her that the investigators from the FBI were trying to rule Ted out as a suspect. Her postmarked letters from Ted could represent important evidence and perhaps prove Ted's innocence by establishing, for example, that he was in Montana on the same day the Unabomber had mailed a bomb from the West Coast. The investigators had lots of questions and were leaving no stone unturned. They had a psychological profile of the Unabomber.

"Well, Dave, I trust your judgment. If you think I should meet with them, then I will. When do they want to see me?"

"Actually, they're waiting downstairs in the parking lot," I had to tell her. "They'd like to talk to you now."

It must have felt to Mom as if her world had come unhinged.

I called Special Agent Kathleen Puckett on her cell phone and buzzed her in. When I opened the apartment door, I could see her coming up the stairs, with agents Lee Stark and Molly Flynn following close behind.

"I don't know what any of this is about," Mom announced as they came in.

What kind of training do FBI agents receive, if any, to help them deal with situations like this? How do you talk to a mother whose son is under investigation without making it seem like an inquisition? In any case, Kathleen, Lee, and Molly handled the situation gracefully. They were polite, professional, even sensitive in the way they approached her, careful to respect her opinions and feelings. They had no search warrant, no legal means to compel her cooperation. I'd told them I wasn't sure but I thought Mom would cooperate.

After explaining a little about the investigation and its methods, Kathleen asked for Mom's help. "Mrs. Kaczynski, do you have anything that might help us carry this investigation forward? Letters from your son, family photographs, anything typewritten that your son might have sent you?" (They were hoping to find a typescript that would match the manual typewriter that was used to produce the manifesto.)

Mom acknowledged that she had lots of things they might be interested in. She sent me to her walk-in closet to retrieve an old trunk full of family keepsakes — the same trunk where I'd found Ted's early essay on technology while Mom lay sick in the hospital six weeks earlier. The trunk was quite heavy, so I dragged it from the closet to the middle of the living room floor. After I snapped open the latches and swung open the lid, she got down on her knees to sift through the contents. Lee and Kathleen pointed to items of interest: letters from Ted, which Mom had arranged in chronological order going back to his years at Harvard; Ted's published mathematical papers alongside his grade school report cards; family photographs.

What happens when you put together a mom and family photographs? You get stories. True to form, Mom told stories. Now I heard not only the usual fond reminiscences, but also an effort to advocate and convince, as if to say, *Look, the Kaczynskis are a normal family; we did all these wholesome things that good families do; Teddy was a good kid; look, here's where we took him camping and he caught his first fish; you're not going to find the Unabomber in a family like ours.*

Molly was occupied primarily with cataloguing the items and writing out receipts before she sealed them in plastic evidence bags. The transformation of a mother's cherished memories into evidence in a criminal case had to follow careful protocols.

At one point, Mom reached deep into the trunk and picked up a little blue book to show her guests. "This is Teddy's baby book," she told them. "It's a diary I kept during the first year of his life. Would you like to see it?"

"Yes, ma'am," Lee said. "It might be very helpful."

But before Mom permitted the little book to go into one of the plastic bags, she leafed through it to locate passages relating to Ted's hospital stay at the age of nine months. She desperately wanted the FBI to know about Ted's hospital experience—the trauma that may have caused her son psychological damage in infancy.

As I stood somewhat apart, gazing at my mother on her knees holding up Ted's baby book, trying to make the agents understand what it meant to her, I realized what a painful situation I had put her in. Yet she was handling it all so bravely. She had such faith—faith in Ted's innocence (which I no longer shared), faith in me (without which I could not have endured), and faith in the criminal justice system— that it would seek truth and justice; that even a mother's worried entries in a baby book more than fifty years ago would be regarded as a clue in that search for justice; that compassionate understanding could generate mercy for her son if the worst came to pass.

I still remember the poignancy of Mom's gesture as she held up Ted's baby book. In effect she was saying, *You're looking for the Unabomber and we'll do everything in our power to help you stop the violence. But don't forget for a moment that the person we're delivering to you is a family member, someone we love. It's the little baby that came out of my womb fifty-some years ago, the child and man I've worried about ever since because of his emotional problems, because his little psyche never really healed from that hospital experience. Don't forget for a moment that there is a human dimension to this tragedy.*

It was all over in about four hours. By the end of that time, Mom and I were utterly depleted. After the agents had gone, I asked Mom what she honestly thought. She repeated that she couldn't believe Ted would maliciously harm others. It seemed to me, though, that her voice carried an undertone of doubt.

We sat silent and numb for a few minutes.

"David," Mom said at last. "Do you remember the time your father found a baby rabbit in the backyard?"

I nodded. It had happened about forty years ago, at our home in Evergreen Park.

"You remember, Dad put the baby rabbit in a cage, but Teddy was extremely upset at the sight of a trapped and obviously frightened little animal. He blurted out, 'Oh, let it go! Please, please let it go!' So your father carried the cage to the empty lot across the street and let the baby rabbit go."

I remembered the story pretty well. As a story, it seemed to speak for itself: Ted was a sensitive child capable of empathy for a frightened animal.

In recalling this event, Mom seemed to pose a question: how could such a sensitive and compassionate child turn into a killer? But her story prompted other questions for me: *Would Ted end up like that trapped rabbit? Would this be the fulfillment of his worst fear?*

A WEEK LATER, at the tail end of March, I caught someone going through our garbage at the curbside. It was a middle-aged guy in a stocking cap who shot a guilty look in my direction, then peeled away in a late-model sedan. Not your typical scavenger, I thought.

"Doesn't the FBI trust us?" I wondered aloud to Linda.

"Let's hope it's them," she rejoined.

A few days later, Ted was arrested. It wasn't until the national news came on that it really sank in what had happened. Linda, Mom, and I sat together in front of the TV screen in Mom's living room. We watched a news clip of Ted being led away from his cabin in handcuffs between two federal marshals. He was skin and bones. His face was blotched with soot; his hair and beard were long and scraggly. His clothing was torn and unbelievably filthy. I had never seen a street person who looked in worse shape than Ted did at that moment. On his face was a dazed, almost otherworldly expression.

"My God!" Mom murmured. Whatever shred of hope or denial we may have been clinging to until that moment exploded before our eyes.

Just as shocking was to hear our family name—Kaczynski—repeated over and over on a national news broadcast in connection with horrible crimes. The knowledge we had guarded so closely with the FBI was a secret no longer—and there was no way it could ever go back to being a secret again. Now the whole world knew about Ted Kaczynski, and from this day forward, people wouldn't associate the name Kaczynski with anything good—with the wonderful values and aspirations that Ted and Wanda Kaczynski had instilled in their children. Instead they would associate the name with violence, madness, and murder. I heard my brother labeled as the suspected "terrorist" and "serial murderer." Even if substantively true, these descriptions missed the story behind the story. The truth as I knew it was not so simple.

Mom's doorbell sounded several times. We decided to ignore it, but at last I sidled up to the window and peered out through the drapes. I saw that the parking lot outside Mom's building was filled with milling reporters, satellite trucks, and cameras on tripods. It was a regular media circus, much more than I had expected. *I know this is a big case, but why are they so focused on* us? I wondered.

My answer came a few moments later. It was being reported on television that Kaczynski had apparently been "fingered" (Dan Rather's word) by his own brother, David Kaczynski of Schenectady, New York.

I couldn't believe what I was hearing, because we'd been promised that our role in the investigation would be held in strictest confidence. *No one will ever know, David,* I'd been told.

Why had they lied to me? Why did this additional and utterly unnecessary blow have to fall? Hadn't we sacrificed enough?

But now it was obvious why all the media were there: people all over the world would be curious to have a look at the guy who had ratted out his own brother.

About forty minutes later, we got a phone call from Kathleen. She explained that there had been a leak. The news media had pressured the FBI into making an arrest sooner rather than later. They had tried to reach our lawyer earlier in the day, but he was on vacation. She said Ted was safe — "irate" but calm. Some evidence had already been found in his cabin. She apologized for the breach of confidentiality.

"David, is there anything . . . anything at all we can do for you?"

I couldn't contain myself. "The only thing I'd ever asked of you, you failed to do!" I shouted, and immediately slammed down the receiver.

We set Mom's alarm clock for four the next morning, hoping to catch the media napping and return in peace to our home a few miles away. I don't think Linda, Mom, or I slept a wink.

We were naive to think we could sneak away. No sooner did we step out of Mom's apartment building than the klieg lights came on as if a trap had been sprung. A gaggle of reporters and photographers came running toward us as we hurried to get in my pickup truck.

"Mrs. Kaczynski," someone shouted, "do you think your son is the Unabomber?"

"You people know more than I do," Mom responded.

I drove as calmly as I could through darkened, tree-lined side streets with several cars following before I turned into our driveway at last. Thankfully, the cars didn't follow us up our driveway. The media's feeding frenzy hadn't yet reached its peak.

I remember only bits and pieces from the following days as we were held hostage by a growing crowd of media camped out on our doorstep.

It seemed that everyone in the country with a microphone, camera, or notepad wanted to hear what the Unabomber's family thought; but we were in shock, without any words to express what we were thinking or feeling at the time. For days, we seldom spoke to one another. We'd just lock glances now and then as if to ask, *Are you OK?*

One scene I vividly recall was Linda methodically draping blankets over our ground-floor windows. She did this after a snooping cameraman attempted to film us inside our home through a narrow opening in the drapes.

I remember flattering notes pushed through our mail slot and flower deliveries as reporters attempted to lure us out onto the front porch to capture a snippet of film for the evening newscast. I was reminded of the horror flick *Night of the Living Dead*, in which several frightened people are holed up in a farmhouse as a phalanx of mindless zombies beat incessantly against the exterior walls and boarded-up windows trying to get at the living flesh inside.

As I took stock of our circumstances, I felt as if our entire future had been blotted out. It was certainly going to be different than our past. I didn't know how we'd ever be able to leave our house, let alone move forward with our lives. I'd be a marked man: the brother of a notorious serial killer, and also the guy who had turned in his own brother. People would wonder what kind of family could have produced such a strange and violent criminal, and they'd also feel instinctively repelled by my disloyalty to my brother. Surely Mom, Linda, and I would be shunned.

We were at an impasse with the media: we wouldn't come out of the house as long as they stayed, and they wouldn't leave until we came out. I'd rather have walked through fire than face those cameras. Beyond that, the future was unimaginable.

Sometimes we'd turn on the TV only to see our house pictured with a reporter in the foreground informing viewers that there was "still no sign of life" inside. Talking heads speculated about our motives. A debate emerged locally about the media's right to be there. A neighbor went on national television to say that we were good people who deserved to be left alone. A local radio host concluded that of course I'd turned in my brother for the reward money—that anyone who imagined otherwise would have to be utterly naive.

I remember vowing to myself, *I will never, ever talk publicly about any of this.* Silence felt like the only piece of integrity I had left. Again and again on the television screen we saw Ted being arrested—his tattered clothing; the bemused, somewhat disconnected look on his face. I wondered how he was being treated and tried to imagine what he must be feeling. Yet we were separated by worlds, locked in separate prisons and separate hells.

From what we could glean from news broadcasts, the evidence taken from Ted's cabin left little doubt that he was the Unabomber.

Linda called various family members and friends to let them know we were OK—at least as OK as we could be. The Schenectady police department could not legally dislodge the reporters from our sidewalk, but after a few days they made the reporters stay out of our yard, which left us feeling a little less vulnerable. The zombies were no longer pounding on our walls, but they were still cluttering the sidewalk and sleeping in cars parked the entire length of our block.

After about a week, Linda heard someone tapping on our back window just after dark. It had been days now since reporters milled around our backyard, so Linda took a chance. She put her face against the window and asked who was there. It was Molly, the FBI agent from Washington.

Linda let Molly in. It was a relief for us to again experience the presence of a human being from outside our little family.

In the middle of our dining room, surrounded by Mom, Linda, and me, Molly started to speak but was unable to get out more than a few words. Attempting to express how terrible she felt about our situation, about the leaks, about the media's unrelenting pressure, about the mob of reporters gathered outside, she couldn't go on. Her shoulders shook uncontrollably in silent sobs as Mom, Linda, and I tried to comfort her, eventually folding her in a group hug.

"It's OK, Molly, it's OK," Mom said soothingly.

TWO YEARS LATER, Ted's trial ended abruptly with a plea bargain that spared his life while condemning him to life imprisonment with no chance of parole.

The next day, Mom and I were ushered into a meeting room at the Federal Building in Sacramento. In the middle of the room were five upholstered chairs arranged in a circle. Sitting in three of the chairs were the widow of a man my brother had killed, her sister, and her late husband's sister.

The three women stood up as we entered the room. Almost in unison, Mom and I said the only thing we could have said under the circumstances: "We're sorry. We're so, so sorry."

However deeply we felt these words, they had a hollow, helpless ring: they were still just words, unable to undo any of the harm that Ted had done to these people. I noticed a tear rolling down Mom's cheek.

After we sat down, the widow spoke first: "We may never meet again in this lifetime. We didn't want to miss this opportunity to speak with you and to tell you how deeply we appreciate what you did. Please convey our thanks to Linda as well. It must have been incredibly difficult to turn in a family member in a case like this. I can't imagine how painful it must have been."

The widow's expression of gratitude came so unexpectedly that it left me speechless. Next to me, I heard Mom murmuring: "We're sorry. We're sorry."

After a pause, the widow continued: "We also want you to know that all we ever wanted was for the violence to stop." I believe this was her way of saying they hadn't wanted the death penalty for Ted.

I don't clearly remember all that followed. I hugged the victim's sister at one point. All five of us were crying, or at least teary-eyed. As survivors of tragedy, we had much in common.

But the mood changed dramatically when Mom started talking about Ted's schizophrenia. Unbeknownst to me, she had come to the meeting with an agenda of her own.

Now looking into the faces of three women whose lives had been utterly devastated by her son's violence, she felt a deep need to help them see her son not as a monster but as a very, very sick man. She needed them to appreciate that it was the illness — not Ted himself — that had done this terrible thing. Although no one had whispered a word about Ted, she desperately wanted her son's victims to understand him rather than hate him. If she could somehow make them see that Ted was sick, it would mean far more to her than being thanked or having her own pain acknowledged.

Over the previous year, she had read and learned a great deal about schizophrenia. Now she wanted her son's victims to learn about it too.

I saw the widow stiffen. Instead of generating understanding as Mom intended, her words were producing pain. Mom was trying to tell her one thing, but what she heard was someone making excuses for the man who had murdered her husband.

Mom's lecture was cut short when the widow abruptly broke in: "He knew what he was doing!" she said severely.

Suddenly the room was frozen in silence.

Five people had followed their best instincts to arrive at a place where reconciliation and some measure of healing had seemed possible. But now the aspiration and the journey appeared futile. There was no point in arguing about Ted's illness.

Across an immense gulf of pain and loss, we saw the faces of people on the other side, but there was no bridge that could carry us across—no way for Mom to completely understand what the widow was feeling, or for the widow to completely understand what Mom was feeling. Each could empathize with the other to a degree, but not enough to overcome the distance. The opportunity to meet and speak had changed nothing.

Meeting like this was a big mistake, I thought. *If only there were some way to leave the room gracefully.*

Mom looked down at the floor, her small body hunched over.

After a moment, she said woodenly: "I wish he had killed me instead of your husband."

I glanced at the widow's face. As she processed Mom's words, I saw the look of hardness slowly melt, replaced by an expression of concern. She sat quietly for a moment, then gently eased herself down from her chair and knelt directly in front of Mom, looking up into her face. The widow's eyes were once again brimming with tears. She was a mother, too. On that very simple human level, she could relate.

With quiet urgency, she said, "Mrs. Kaczynski, you don't deserve any of this. Don't ever imagine that we blame you. It's not your fault. You have nothing to blame yourself for. You don't deserve this burden."

OUR FATHER, Theodore R. Kaczynski, passed away half a decade before Ted's arrest. On one hand, Mom and Linda and I were grateful that he was spared the ordeal we had to endure. On the other hand, his absence left us with a feeling of incompleteness at a time we needed strength. Moreover, the circumstances of his death were traumatic.

In the late fall of 1990, Dad committed suicide with a .22-caliber rifle—a weapon he had seldom used but had occasionally allowed me to shoot when I was a boy. He had been diagnosed with terminal cancer, which offered an explanation for his decision to take his own life. He was, among other things, a pragmatist with no belief in or fear of an afterlife. In his personal search for truth, he elevated reason above intuition and emotion. He viewed self-deception as the consummate folly.

Looking back, I saw plenty of signs that he had made up his mind to end his life. But I never saw it coming. Newly married, I'd taken a leave of absence from my job in New York to provide support for Dad and Mom in Chicago. I drove Dad to the hospital for his daily radiation treatments. We had good talks. Although I saw him struggling at times to control his emotions, I never realized he was trying to tell me goodbye.

Early one morning on the eve of my birthday I heard a sharp sound. A few moments later, Mom opened the door to my bedroom and said in a worried voice, "Dave, your father has fallen. He doesn't seem able to get up."

I rushed down the hallway to my parents' bedroom. Mom had gotten up earlier, had been puttering around in the kitchen when we heard the sound. I switched on the light and saw Dad lying beside the bed on the wooden floor, where dark blood was beginning to pool. Some long object was sticking out from under his body. My first half-conscious thought was that his cane had broken and that one splintered end had stabbed him, causing a serious wound. But in the next second I realized that the protruding object was a rifle barrel.

"Mom, he shot himself!"

I'd never glimpsed eyes so deeply closed. I knew in that instant that Dad was never coming back. I pressed my mouth close to his ear, desperate to say goodbye.

"Father, I love you, I love you! Father, I love you!" I hoped he might still be able to hear something.

Mom's reaction was very different. She hit his lifeless body, whacking him hard several times. "We had time left!" she cried. "I wanted to care for you!"

To her, Dad's suicide was a betrayal. Married to this man for fifty-one years, she'd expected a fuller, more tender, less self-centered goodbye.

For me, the questions began in earnest when we realized after a cursory search that Dad had left no suicide note. Had he taken his life on a sudden impulse? Or because of depression?

I didn't tell Mom that Dad had taken advantage of our last few days together to tell me goodbye in several ways. He had said, "David, you're the best son I could have wished for." He'd given me his father's gold watch the night before. He'd also said, "I'm glad you're here to support your mother."

"But Dad, I'm here for you, too!" I'd said, never guessing that within twelve hours he'd be gone.

Within twenty-four hours, Mom was rehearsing a narrative that was to be her cover story for the next twenty years: Dad was a hero who saved us and himself months of suffering and needless expense. His suicide was an act of courage motivated by reason and generosity.

She was reluctant to bring his clothing to the Salvation Army as long as it retained a trace of his scent. As if by force of will, she repressed her resentment over the way he had left her. (Linda made me swear never to do what my father had done, which was not difficult for me after seeing how Dad's suicide affected Mom.) She began to tout Dr. Kevorkian as a political hero and to blame religious conservatism for depriving her and Dad of an opportunity to share a proper and meaningful goodbye.

Linda expressed concern that if Mom moved too soon to New York to be close to us, her emotional needs might consume me and possibly disrupt our fledgling marriage. Yet I felt misgivings about leaving her behind in Chicago, since she'd already been abandoned by one son and, in a sense, by her husband as well. She had never been a gregarious sort. Her emotional life had revolved around her family. How would she sustain herself now?

I learned how resilient she was barely two weeks later. She told me that she had taken a part-time job as a playground monitor at a nearby elementary school. Over the next five years I heard descriptions and stories of all the children she interacted with there. She was especially sensitive to kids who were bullied or socially isolated. When Linda and I visited our families at Thanksgiving and Christmas, we always found her fridge covered with cheerful pictures, greetings, and cards the children had drawn and written for her. In the depths of her grief, she had recommitted herself to life.

In later years, I visited Mom routinely on Sunday afternoons at her nearby apartment at a senior citizen complex in Schenectady. There wasn't a lot for us to talk about. I wasn't interested in discussing my job on my days off and by then Mom's experience of the world was limited to news received from visitors to her small apartment. She would report on her conversations with her home health care aides about their children, their aspirations and backgrounds. Otherwise, I would read the Sunday newspaper, take a nap on the couch, or join Mom in watching a bit of TV. I'd learned that my mere presence was sufficient to bring her comfort; anything I might add in the way of personal sharing was strictly a bonus from her point of view.

Sometimes I brought Mom little treats. She loved nuts, so one afternoon when I came to visit I cheerfully announced, "Mom, I got you a can of cashews!"

By then her hearing was not so good. She looked up at me in astonishment. "What? You got a tattoo?"

I never thought Mom was capable of acknowledging to herself, let alone to anyone else, her true feelings regarding her husband's suicide. But a remarkable thing happened in the spring of 2010, twenty years after Dad's suicide and fifteen months before Mom's death. One late spring evening I was about to take my leave when, out of the blue, Mom began to talk about her feelings regarding Dad's illness and death.

"After your father died, David, I searched all over the house for a note. I just couldn't understand why he didn't say goodbye to me."

"Maybe he couldn't find the words to say goodbye."

"It wouldn't have taken much. Just the words 'I love you' would have been enough. After I realized there was no note, I began looking all around the house for a sign of some kind, some indication that he wanted me to know that he loved me. Anything at all. I didn't know what I was looking for, but I thought I'd recognize it when I saw it. But again, nothing."

"You know, Mom, Dad was never comfortable with strong emotions. I always thought of you as a feeling person, a passionate person, whereas Dad was more drawn to wisdom, which involves a certain distance. Maybe in that extreme situation his emotions overwhelmed him, left him incapable of expressing the thoughts and feelings he did have."

"Yes, but there were times when I felt his rejection. Do you remember when Stella and Ralph came to visit after Dad's diagnosis? We were all sitting in the living room. I'd moved my chair close to Dad's, and at one point I reached out to clasp his hand, but instead of holding my hand, he brusquely pulled his hand away. I felt so hurt."

"Well, maybe Dad was at a stage where he needed to let go of life instead of clinging to it. Holding your hand would have been a painful reminder — maybe too painful to bear — of all he was about to leave behind. Mom, I *know* Dad loved you."

"I know he did too. But remember that I lived with him for more than fifty years. I could read his feelings to a certain extent. In the last two weeks, I felt a kind of coldness coming from him. And within that coldness, I know, there was anger and resentment.

"I think the source of his anger and resentment was jealousy that I would continue living, that our family life would go on, that we would continue to celebrate holidays, maybe for years to come. That I would get to know Linda as a daughter-in-law, and that there might even be a grandchild for me to dote on, a grandchild he would never see.

"Of course, the future didn't turn out to be so rosy. We didn't know about the tragedy that you and Linda and I would have to face, and I'm not sure Dad could have handled it. I'm afraid it would have destroyed him.

"David, don't worry. Don't be sad. I've forgiven Dad with all my heart. He was who he was—a human being with limitations as well as wonderful qualities. I wish our life together had ended differently, but I loved him deeply and always will."

AS MOM LAY ON her deathbed, I felt the need to reach out to Ted. He deserved a chance to come out of his emotional prison, to reconcile and heal what might well have been the primary relationship of his life. And I knew that nothing could possibly mean more to Mom than to hear Ted's voice again, to know that her love—and all the complicated emotions bound up with it, the unique bond between two extraordinary people—was acknowledged in the end.

In some ways, Ted represented her life's aspiration gone terribly awry. There was no way to settle her many questions about him, no way to know whether the naive egoism of her aspiration had damaged Ted in any way—whether her grand hopes for her children had contributed to a grand tragedy—and no way to redo any of it. In the bond between parent and child there is always a great gulf, an unaccountable element of difference or hidden karma that will inevitably translate the family dynamic into a wider arena. It could be that behind every great person or villain there is a powerful, resonant parent-child relationship.

I don't know exactly how I fit into the picture. Perhaps no one can see his own role clearly from inside a complex family structure. Sometime during the last year of her life, during one of those Sunday afternoons in her apartment, Mom said, "David, when you were born, I had this strong intuition that you had come to save us."

I can honestly say that I never felt the burden of that expectation while growing up. Perhaps it was what the psychologists call a "backformation"—a matter of Mom reconstructing her life's narrative from some later vantage point. But it's intriguing to reflect that even at that early stage—her firstborn just seven years old—Mom may have had a hunch her family needed saving.

Now I certainly *did* feel the burden. I'd gotten used to the way things were, which meant that for many years Ted had been remote and unavailable, far closer in my memories than in reality.

I couldn't let Mom know I planned to call the prison. I found it hard to believe that Ted might actually respond, so to kindle Mom's hope at this late stage would have been too cruel. Did Mom know I would try to reach Ted? I imagine so. Was she resigned to having lost Ted? Is such resignation ever complete?

The first person I reached at the prison, a switchboard operator, promptly connected me with a prison chaplain. To me her voice sounded less like a chaplain's than a correctional officer's, intent on establishing a firm boundary, accustomed to putting up a bureaucratic front. I started to explain the purpose of my call, trying to penetrate the walls of a fortress with my human need.

I had delivered the news about Mom's failing health to various family members and to Mom's closest friends. In doing so, I'd never lost my composure or shed a tear. But now I was speaking to someone who would convey the message directly to my brother.

"Nothing," I explained to the chaplain, "would mean more to her . . ." but at that point I broke down sobbing, unable to go on. I might have been thinking how much it would mean to Mom to hear from Ted. Or that Ted was being offered a chance — one irrecoverable chance — to make his own heart whole.

The chaplain's voice softened. "Take your time," she said.

By fits and starts, I got out what I had to say. The chaplain assured me that there would be no problem with putting Ted on the phone with his mother if it could be verified that she was close to death. I provided her with a phone number for Mom's doctor. The chaplain said she would go at once to speak with Ted.

I heard nothing back for two days. I wasn't exactly on tenterhooks: Linda and I were deeply occupied with keeping Mom as comfortable as we could.

A few days before she died, an aide put Mom in a wheelchair and brought her to her living room. Everyone had given up on keeping Mom alive except her aides, who regularly plied her with sunny talk and offers of food. By this point Mom had forgotten her resolve to stop eating and drinking, yet she couldn't manage to swallow the tiny bit of yogurt the aide had spooned into her mouth. Getting her bearings, Mom gazed around her living room as if at some unfamiliar sight. "How long have I been here?" she wondered.

"Mom, you've been living here for ten years," I told her.

"Ten years?" she said in great surprise. "Ten years?" She repeated the words several times over with deepening incredulity. Life was such a mystery!

The chaplain never called me back. Perhaps Ted had forbidden her to do so. In any case, Mom's doctor relayed a message from the prison chaplain: Ted did not want to speak with his mother. So that was it.

MOM'S EARLY VISION FOR her sons remains clear in my mind: we would develop intelligence and compassion and use our intelligence, guided by our compassion, to benefit humanity. This mission would form the basis of our personal integrity, providing us with the courage needed to make unconventional or difficult choices.

I remember that Mom pronounced the word "integrity" with reverence.

But the reality of life's journey, with its many obstacles and tests, is not so easy to formulate. In some ways Ted never stopped being his mother's son. Unfortunately, his capacity for empathy was eroded by his strong sense of personal injury and disappointment; his hope for the world was shattered by an apocalyptic vision. His sense of utter helplessness in the face of the overwhelming threat technology posed to wild nature and to human freedom upset his fragile equilibrium and drove him to resist through violent means. He felt compelled to speak his truth; his integrity depended on it. He posed questions— important questions about humanity's future—that no one who has

truly understood them can answer. Yet his questions go largely un-
heard because of (among other things) the deafening violence that
accompanied them.

I SEE THE KACZYNSKI family as holding certain symmetries. For as
far back as I can remember, we were paired up based on certain simi-
larities and differences in our looks and temperaments. Dad and I had
lighter hair and brown eyes; Mom and Ted had dark hair and blue
eyes. Dad and I were more social and easygoing; Mom and Teddy
tended to be anxious and somewhat withdrawn. On the other hand,
Dad and Ted both expressed a strong commitment to reason over
emotion, whereas Mom and I (increasingly as I grew older) tended
to trust intuition over analysis. When upset, Mom and I reacted emotionally and then mostly got over it, whereas Dad and Ted (increasingly as he grew older) tended to withdraw. Dad, unless you count
his suicide, never lashed out; Ted, after nursing his wounds through
years of silence, lashed out in a big, big way, expressing his pent-up
rage through angry, hyperbolic letters that marred his parents' happiness, and finally through murderous bombs accompanied by elaborate (I want to say "tortured") justifications.

When I was young, I tended to see Mom as the outlier. In contrast
to Dad and Teddy (and me too, as a would-be member of a conven-
tionally male club that prized rationality over feeling), Mom at times
celebrated strong emotions.

My most vivid memory of this comes from a family vacation we
took when I was in middle school. On a long drive to some forest
camping spot in another state, Mom began to expound with enthu-
siasm on the classical Greek tragedies. She was fresh from reading
Sophocles's *Antigone*. Mom explained the drama's plot, which entailed
suicides, a sibling rivalry, an intense conflict between Antigone's sense
of justice and the law, and a blood bond stronger than life itself. I
found the story inexplicable and troubling. Antigone's irrational need

to sacrifice her own life in defense of her dead brother's honor seemed gratuitous, disproportional. It accomplished nothing; it only spread more misery. At every turn and twist of the story, I thought there surely could have been a way out of fate's trap, if only the characters had had the foresight and sense to make rational choices.

I remember that Dad at some point lit a cigarette (one of the thousands that would eventually doom him) and Teddy rolled down his window and waved the smoke outside with exaggerated gestures. I wanted to do the same with *Antigone*.

How could Mom find nobility in such conflict and violence? Mom's emotional exuberance clashed with my need for emotional stability, my grounding in what I regarded as reality.

How could following one's principles lead to disaster? How could Antigone's (or anyone's) vital life force be converted into a death force?

I tried to be dismissive: Mom was a female given to emotional excess; the story took place a long, long time ago; it was, after all, *just* a story. What could it possibly have to do with us?

MOM HAS BEEN GONE since 2011. I still feel a great sense of loss, although I can easily remember her voice and face as vividly as when she was alive. I feel some tension between my belief that everything is impermanent and my intuition that nothing is — especially the love between individual human beings.

Buddhist tradition teaches that all things are impermanent except the capacity to become enlightened — a potential that exists within all sentient beings without exception, from the tiniest microbe to human beings. The Judeo-Christian tradition embraces the image of an afterlife where all humans are potentially redeemable, where all that has been lost will be made whole. So I am still working out a tension between my Buddhist path and my Western intuition of the eternal.

Both Buddhists and Judeo-Christians, to my understanding, adhere to a linear sense of time that spans the distant past to the distant future, moving ever forward. It took an atheistic Western philosopher, Friedrich Nietzsche, to posit a circular sense of time, which he named the Eternal Recurrence of the Same. Perhaps I could sum up Nietzsche's theory by saying that what happened once simply *is*, forever.

On the first anniversary of my mother's death, I placed various pictures on my Buddhist altar to memorialize our relationship: Mom holding a smiling baby that once was me, Mom and a scruffy-looking adolescent (me) sitting on a bench near the site of my college graduation, Mom and me seated side by side on a couch in her living room a couple of years before her death.

Does it make sense to say that "I" live on when in truth I look so different from those images of "me" captured in the past? What strikes me as far more real is the invisible bond linking two human beings over sixty-two years.

According to Buddhist doctrine, my mother has been reborn somewhere by now. The thought inspires me to pray that all little children in the world are fortunate enough to have the love and protection Mom and Dad gave to Ted and me.

Ted Sr., Teddy, and Wanda, ca. 1944

Davy, Wanda, and Teddy in Chicago duplex, 1949

Ted Sr., Davy, and Wanda, ca. 1950

Wanda, Teddy, Ted Sr., and Davy outside family home in Evergreen Park, 1952

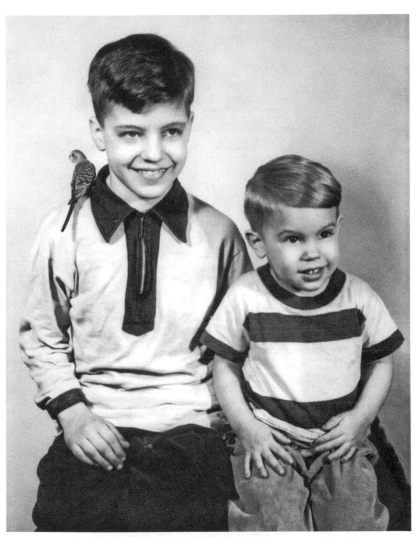

Teddy with parakeet and David, 1952

Ted Sr., Davy, and Teddy on family outing to forest preserve, 1953

Teddy's school picture, ca. 1953

Mom, Davy, and Teddy, ca. 1953

Davy, Ted Sr., and Teddy on camping trip, ca. 1954

Teddy, Ted Sr., and Davy on camping trip, ca. 1954

Teddy, cousin Kathy, Aunt Josephine, David, Ted Sr., and
Uncle Stanley, ca. 1956

David and Teddy, "Siamese twins," ca. 1958

Teddy graduates from high school, 1958

Teddy leaves for Harvard, 1958

Kaczynski family home in Evergreen Park, 1950s

David in Little League uniform, 1959

Dave and Ted in Lisbon, Iowa, 1966

Mom and Ted cooking over campfire, ca. 1966

Ted in front of his cabin in Montana, 1972

Ted on Montana land, 1973

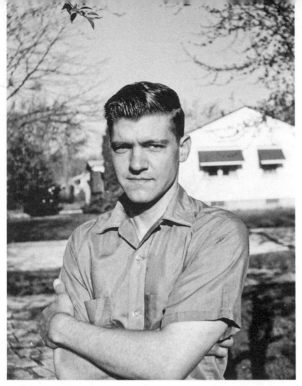

Ted, Lombard, Illinois, 1978

Dave, Mom, and Ted Sr., Lombard, Illinois, 1978

Teddy reading in Lombard living room, 1979

Ted in Montana, last visit from his parents, 1982

Dave, Mom, and Linda, Christmas in Lombard, 1989

Dave, Dad, and Linda, Christmas in Lombard, 1989

Linda and Dave at backyard wedding, Schenectady, New York, July 14, 1990

Dave and Mom, Schenectady, July 14, 1990

Dave writing in cabin in Big Bend, Texas, 1991

< CHAPTER 3 >

GHOST WITHIN ME

I STRUGGLE TO REMEMBER my father—so much has happened since he left the world a quarter century ago.

In place of memories, I feel his presence as a steady emotional warmth, like a cast-iron stove heated by long-burning coals.

I can distinctly visualize his brown eyes darting from side to side — like the rapid eye movements of a dreamer—when he searched for words to express a thought, or when he immersed himself in memories.

AT AN EARLY AGE I BECAME fascinated with baseball and convinced my parents to sign me up for a youth summer league. At a preseason gathering of fathers, Dad was pressed into service to manage a team. The only problem was that he knew next to nothing about baseball. Dad enjoyed telling his friends how one of the boys on the team had approached him after our second game and handed him a baseball instruction book, saying, "Here, Mr. K, maybe this will help."

Having Dad as my team's manager turned out to be somewhat awkward for us both. I sensed that Dad disapproved of my ambition and my appetite for competition. Meanwhile, I tried to take advantage of Coach Dad by bugging him to let me pitch. I grew frustrated when he pointed out that another boy had more talent as a pitcher. Eventually I wore him down and he gave me a chance to pitch, which I promptly squandered by walking six batters in a row before he yanked me. Somehow, despite Dad's deficiencies and mine, we ended the season tied for first place.

I turned out to be an excellent first baseman and a fair hitter. I was even selected for the league's all-star team. The last, crucial game of the season ended with some drama: the game was tied and the bases loaded with two outs in the bottom of the last inning.

We all groaned as we realized that it was Bobby's turn to bat. Bobby was a terrible hitter who had struck out every single time at bat that season.

"Take me out, Mr. K!" Bobby pleaded.

Dad shook his head. "No, you go ahead, Bobby. You can do it!"

Somehow Bobby managed to draw a walk that pushed in the winning run. He ran to first base and jumped up and down on the bag in pure joy. We all crowded around him in celebration. Afterward Dad made a little speech to the team that included praise for Bobby's determination and courage. Days later, he talked about Bobby to a group of his friends.

It dawned on me that Dad's pride in my talent and success was overshadowed by his compassion and admiration for the underdog Bobby.

AS I ADVANCED TO Little League, even Teddy, who tended to avoid public settings, would sometimes come to the park to watch me play, sitting side by side with Dad in the bleachers. Since my brother didn't seem interested in baseball and tended to disdain activities that didn't interest him, I guessed that he came to my ball games because he enjoyed watching me play, which both pleased and surprised me. When he learned to drive at age sixteen, he would sometimes drive me to baseball practices.

One night after a game, a slender, dark-haired, very pretty little girl came up to where I stood alone behind the backstop. I was shy around girls, so I was a little taken aback when she looked me directly in the eyes and said, "You pitch good!"

I didn't know how to answer her. What could I say? I'd just finished pitching the worst game that had ever been pitched in the history of baseball. I'd given up thirteen runs in one inning; my team lost badly. Now here was this cute girl saying, *Hey, you pitch good!*

"Thanks," I mumbled, not knowing what else to say.

"Say, could you give me a dime? I need a dime for some fries," she said. I fished a dime out of my jeans pocket and handed it over, and the girl sped off toward the concession stand.

I know for sure that Linda and I met about a year later, at the start of seventh grade. We were thrown together in an accelerated class for the school's brightest students. Linda had already skipped a grade. She was dark-haired, slender, and pretty.

Only years later did I connect Linda with my memory of the girl at the baseball field. She lived close by, she reminded me. She and her younger sister Gail used to frequent the baseball field on game nights, bumming small change that they would quickly convert into ice cream and fries.

Had that very sympathetic and opportunistic girl of my early memories been Linda? Was this the first meeting of two people who would later become linked in friendship, love, and marriage? Was it my first encounter with a person who would one day solve a momentous riddle and leave both our lives changed forever?

Was Ted at the baseball field that night when I probably had my first encounter with Linda? I think so. But I find it impossible to answer these questions with certainty. They test the reliability of my memories, and also remind me of the connecting threads that hold remembered events in a series through time, turning our lives into narrative—or many possible alternative narratives.

If Ted was not there that night, walking me back to the car, awkwardly placing a comforting hand on my shoulder, commenting on my dismal performance—"That's really tough"—then it was some other night. It was still my brother and me, and the emotional significance was the same.

DAD WORKED HARD without ever trying to advance himself. For thirty years, he made sausages at his uncle's store in Chicago. He was a blue-collar intellectual. Though he didn't have much formal education, he was widely read and believed progress was possible through mankind's rational pursuit of the greater good. When I was only a small boy, he explained to me the meaning of the phrase "enlightened self-interest."

In the 1950s, he played a key role in reforming the village school board to eliminate the influence of partisan politics. For a couple of years, a number of men and some women from our community regularly gathered at our home to discuss a progressive agenda for the school system. Dad was always patient but persistent—a voice of reason whenever feelings ran high and disagreements flared toward animosity.

Once he invited U.S. Senator Paul Douglas, a noted liberal, to speak in Evergreen Park, a Republican stronghold, on the need for federal aid to education. After the event Senator Douglas—who had had to field a number of hostile questions—approached Dad and said, "Ted, I hope I didn't get you into trouble."

"Not at all." Dad smiled; he didn't seem to mind what some of our small-minded neighbors thought.

Our parents, despite their different personalities, held fundamentally similar views, especially when it came to education, politics, and issues related to their children's welfare. They taught us about civil disobedience — explained that transcendent ethical principles could be invoked to override a bad law. They admired the civil rights activists in the South who endured arrest and jail to awaken the nation's conscience against racial injustice. At the same time, they believed that enlightened citizenship meant following the law as an individual commitment to the social compact — that finding a particular law disagreeable or inconvenient was not enough to justify disobeying it. Otherwise our democracy, subverted by individual whims, would crumble.

I was about ten or eleven one Fourth of July when I begged my father for permission to buy some firecrackers. Most of my friends had them. I only wanted a few small ones, I explained.

"Dad, they're safe." I pleaded. "I'll be really careful. I promise I'll wear sunglasses to protect my eyes."

I never feared Dad as a disciplinarian. Discipline in our family was based on reason and dialogue, not authority and fear. I knew from experience that my father could be flexible if I approached him in the right way. I could be very persuasive. All other things being equal, Dad preferred to accommodate.

On the subject of firecrackers, however, he wouldn't budge. "Dave, they're illegal," he said. "It's a matter of principle that we respect the law. Just because you want something is never enough reason to break the law."

I detected a certain familiar firmness in his voice, and of course I heard that fateful word "principle." It was a compelling word, referencing great ideas contained in humanistic books and the Declaration of Independence. I knew my cause was lost.

GROWING UP, I NEVER doubted for a moment that my parents loved me. I never questioned that the four members of our family were connected through unbreakable bonds of love. Only as I neared adolescence did I realize that Dad's relationship with Ted was different than his relationship with me. Years later, a therapist I was seeing attempted to shed some light on the difference.

However unconditional a parent's love might be, she said, it's nigh impossible to continue loving a child who doesn't love back. Ted didn't return our parents' love — at least not in ways that were easy to recognize or receive. When hugged as a child, he squirmed instead of hugging back. Later on in adolescence, he stiffened when being hugged by his mother. It was as if Ted's way of relating obeyed a different set of rules. Unable to fathom Ted's internal physics, Dad eventually gave up, whereas Mom preferred to believe that Ted's sensitive inner self was normally loving, only hard to reach (because of his "hospital experience").

Mom and Dad confronted a similar problem when it came to disciplining Ted, who seemed to have more respect for rules than for the relationships they are designed to protect.

One time Ted played a nasty trick on Mom. As she approached the dinner table with a pot of hot spaghetti sauce in hand, Ted made a show of gallantly pulling out a chair for her to sit down in, then jerked the chair back farther as she started to sit, causing her to fall on her butt. Luckily, only her dignity was injured — she even managed to keep from spilling the pot of sauce.

"I could have been hurt!" she howled.

"Go to your room!" Dad shouted. Ted ran to his room, laughing as he ran.

Afterward Mom and Dad locked worried glances across the table. Then they each looked down.

Ted could be made to follow rules for the most part. He was a "good kid" in that sense. But no one could make him feel remorse for having hurt someone's feelings. Sometimes it seemed as if he had a well-developed superego and no heart. Mom and Dad were at a loss about how to deal with this.

They didn't believe in spanking, but Dad spanked Ted once when he was about ten years old. Teddy attended an elementary school about a mile from our home, and by this age he was allowed to walk home from school by himself. We lived in a safe community where crime was virtually unheard-of. One evening, however, Teddy hadn't arrived home by suppertime, which was quite unusual. Mom and Dad grew worried, so Dad drove around and around the neighborhood looking for Teddy, to no avail. Mom called the homes of two of Teddy's little friends and was told that he was not there. By then it was well after dark. Dad went out again, driving slowly along darkened streets, looking for his missing son. Mom put in a call to the police, panic rising in her voice, to find out if any child had been involved in an accident and been taken to a hospital.

Teddy called home around ten that evening. "Come pick me up," he said smugly.

He had gotten his friend to lie to Mom over the telephone. He'd been at his friend's house the whole time. He knew his parents had been frantic, but their distress only seemed to amuse him.

Dad, against his own principles and as a measure of his anger and consternation, took Teddy down in the basement and spanked him hard.

The next day Teddy's manner was transformed to one of uncharacteristic meekness and mildness. He seemed chastened. Possibly my brother—"abandoned" to a hospital as an infant—received his spanking as a form of reassurance that he was loved. Or perhaps it comforted him to have his sense of order and equilibrium restored through justice—due administration of a deserved punishment.

THE KACZYNSKI HOME WAS almost always filled with music, either recorded or homemade. When the local classical music station wasn't on, Teddy played his trombone or I practiced my trumpet. When I grew older and more adept, Teddy presented duets for us to play together, some of which he'd written himself. Like many people gifted in mathematics, Teddy also had a gift for music. After Dad bought a piano (he'd learned to play in early adulthood), Ted would sometimes sit at the piano for hours composing counterpoint in the style of the baroque masters. I couldn't tell whether my brother was going to be the next Einstein or the next Bach. I remember the deep sense of belonging I felt on occasions when Dad, Teddy, and I would play music together, sometimes joined by Mom, who had a beautiful singing voice. Our family quartet represented a perfect metaphor of the spiritual attunement that defined our family — or so I imagined.

DAD HAD A FEW CLOSE, lifelong friends. But he was also a gadfly of sorts. When we went camping, Mom, Ted, and I would typically keep our distance from other campers, while Dad inevitably wandered around the campground striking up conversations with anyone he could find. It was the same in our hometown: on summer nights and weekends, when he wasn't working around the house, Dad would stroll up and down the block to gab and share news with our neighbors. Women especially loved his easygoing ways. His friend Ralph once told me that Dad possessed some magic that made him irresistible to women and the envy of all his male friends. He never did stop flirting with members of the opposite sex, but he settled down after marrying Mom and remained a faithful husband.

He must have wondered about his sons. We never dated. I had been a cheerful child, but I grew more inward and introverted in adolescence. Ted and I both received an Ivy League education, but neither of us turned that education into a respectable, middle-class job. And although Ted was handy like Dad, I never was. Instead of engaging with the material world, I grew more and more interested in abstract philosophy. Dad was intelligent, curious, and open-minded. He enjoyed learning from others, but I'm afraid our conversations on literature and philosophy often left him puzzled.

When I moved away in my early thirties to live in the Texas desert, Dad seemed to take vicarious enjoyment in my adventure. He was eager to learn about my improvised earth dwelling and told me the early French trappers had a name for that kind of an earthen dugout—they called it an *abri*. So a year later, on his first visit to my ten-acre plot in the middle of nowhere, he expressed eagerness to see the place where I camped.

I led him on a winding path through a low growth of brambles and shrubs to my *abri*. It was just a rectangular hole in the ground slightly larger than an open grave, partly sheltered under pieces of corrugated tin. Dad stood there looking down into the hole for a minute or two, clearly troubled by what he saw. He said nothing. I imagine he expected to find a domicile less crude, more ingeniously designed—something he might later enjoy describing to his friends. I sensed that in looking down into the hole he was also experiencing a hole in his heart, a sudden sense of loss, a worry that all was not right with his putatively normal son.

Nevertheless, in the years that followed, I felt his influence keeping me company as I made a life for myself in nature. If you really want to experience the night sky, retire to the desert, where the sky is clear and the air is dry, where the stars appear in greater number and with astonishing vividness.

On a typical, quiet evening, I'd cook my dinner of rice and beans at sunset over an open campfire, often remembering our family vacations spent camping in Wisconsin or Michigan, and once in the Smoky Mountains of Appalachia.

Two things I remember about Dad from these early trips: he loved peering into the flames of a campfire, and he loved gazing up at the star-filled sky. Now in Texas I could do both to my heart's content.

To Dad, both the fire gazing and the stargazing were forms of contemplation, the former focused on the mind and memory, the latter on the vastness of the universe beyond our ken. He discovered a sense of wonder in both. In the desert, I revisited those senses of wonder night after night, often thanking Dad for having introduced me to them.

Dad was big on sharing. "Dave," he said more than once, "an experience not shared is never full or complete. There's something missing when we're all alone, don't you think?"

But I couldn't agree with him. When it came to certain kinds of experiences, especially those I regarded as spiritual, subjectivity was paramount in my view. To me the presence of another human being—however much loved—was inevitably a subtraction. In this way, I was like Ted.

Night after night, year after year for eight years, I'd sit by the campfire all alone, sometimes joined by my memories of people, but fundamentally apart, never in actual company, turning absence into a positive, holding in balance the vastness of the universe beyond with the vastness of the universe within.

My brother, I assumed, was engaged in similar reveries a thousand miles to the north. It would have bowled me over to learn that he was engaged instead in meticulous bomb making, night after night, weaving his resentment of technological society into a campaign of terror. How different we really were I could not then have imagined.

EARLY ON, I MADE SUMMER visits to my parents' home outside Chicago to play in an organized softball league and to earn a little money as a bus driver. In the latter years of my Texas sojourn, I only visited Mom and Dad for about two weeks at Christmastime.

The last time Ted visited home, around 1980, he and Dad went on a two-week camping trip together in northern Minnesota. Although I never put it into words for myself, I really hoped that Dad and Ted might forge a deeper bond. Perhaps what had been missing in their father-son relationship could be partly reclaimed, if not discovered for the first time. But it was never to be. Dad reported that it had been the longest two weeks of his life. Why? "Because I missed Wanda so much!" Not because his time spent with his son had been difficult, but rather because he had spent very little time with Ted, who'd gone off canoeing by himself in remote backwaters. I should have known that Dad and Ted were two souls on completely different wavelengths.

By contrast, I felt my father's love more deeply during the latter years of his life. One important memory comes to mind. Around Christmastime, my parents always hosted their best friends—a pair of old married couples they'd remained close to for over fifty years. After dinner, the conversation (as usual) waxed philosophical, which provided me with an opening to share some of my developing views. Mom and Dad's friends were good listeners. They asked probing questions. They generously did their best to hear what I was saying, to somehow convert my misty propositions into graspable substance. But it was just no use. They were stuck in Enlightenment rationalism. They weren't prepared to surrender, or even capable of surrendering, the solid ground that supported their understanding of the world. They didn't seem to feel affronted by my challenges to that understanding, only mildly curious and baffled.

As the conversation was winding down, Dad said something that warmed my heart. Even now I remember his words with gratitude. They were both validating and freeing.

"I'm not able to follow most of Dave's ideas," he summed up. "But I have a rather strong intuition that he's onto something significant and meaningful. I do my best to follow where he's leading. It's murky territory for me, but I'm really glad that he's on the journey he's on."

ABOUT TEN YEARS EARLIER, Dad and I spent a week camping and fishing on the Illinois side of the Mississippi River. Although Dad had enjoyed fishing from time to time, I knew that the opportunity to spend some quality time with his son meant more to him than the chance to catch a few fish. This was just a month or two before Linda persuaded me to become a vegetarian, and several years before my exposure to the Texas gun culture turned me against firearms.

One evening, as our day's catch was simmering over the campfire, I asked Dad if he'd care to try hunting with me some time. Pheasant hunting was something I'd tried once, unsuccessfully, with a teacher colleague friend of mine in Iowa. Now the idea of going hunting was just a passing thought that found its way into words at the weary end of an active day. Dad then told me a story I'd never heard before.

"Dave, I only went hunting once. Teddy was a young boy then, eager to come along with me when I went rabbit hunting on Gorem's farm. Teddy was really into it, on the lookout for rabbits as we roamed the grassy fields of Indiana farmland. Finally I spied a rabbit, carefully aimed the shotgun and shot it dead. But as we stood over the dead rabbit, Teddy's mood changed. He seemed crushed to see this once animate, alert creature stretched out lifeless on the ground. 'Oh, the poor, poor bunny!' he wailed. Then he started crying. I felt terrible, reflecting on the pointless killing I had just done and the effect of that senseless deed written on Teddy's face. I vowed that day that I would never go hunting again."

DURING THE LAST YEAR of his life, Dad and I were, without realizing it, at emotional crosscurrents. I was coming out of my desert isolation to marry Linda, to reengage with the world—returning to life, so to speak. Dad, on the other hand, was dying, in the process of detaching from life and letting go.

Once I asked his advice on whether Linda and I should try to have a child. "I wouldn't want to bring a child into the world," he said.

A few days before his death, he offered the following: "Dave, I'm really surprised that you decided to get back in the game."

"What do you mean?"

"I was very surprised you decided to marry, to come back to society. I thought you would spend the rest of your life in the desert."

Although I'd never talked much about Linda, it didn't take a genius to realize that spending the rest of my life with Linda was, for me, the fulfillment of a longtime dream. Everyone could see that I was fairly glowing with happiness. And, as a man happily married for more than fifty years, Dad was in a position to know how fulfilling marriage could be. Had Dad found life so disappointing? Was he projecting his own need for distance and letting-go on me? Did he unconsciously want me to identify with his withdrawal from the world?

Although I was physically present for my father in his last week (and I don't downplay the importance of that), I was unable to be emotionally present for him, since our lives were moving in opposite directions. His suicide came as an utter shock; I had missed all the signs. His reasons left untold, Mom and I were left to mourn and speculate.

I cannot dismiss Mom's long-running story that Dad's suicide was an act of self-sacrifice. From the perspective of a man withdrawing from life, he may well have thought that he was holding me back. I had taken a leave of absence from my job (and from my young marriage) to care for him. I'd put on hold my plans to accompany Linda on her teaching term abroad in Greece a few months hence. The doctors had given him somewhere between three months and three years to live. He might have decided it was time for both of us to "get on with it."

While I was hurt and deeply disappointed by Dad's suicide — especially by his failure to tell Mom he loved her — my brother wrote me a note expressing his admiration for Dad's courage. He said that in "doing what he had to do" our father had shown a lot of guts. Although Ted declined our invitation to attend the memorial service, he made a rare phone call from a pay phone to Mom to convey his sympathy. She sensed that he might have been crying on the other end of the line as he hung up. It was reassuring to know Ted still had feelings for his family.

As for Dad, I know he was proud of his marriage, because he frequently said so. Instead of passion or romance, he referenced the commonality of values that linked him with another human being over fifty years. He and Mom were like-minded about nearly everything they thought important—ethics, education, politics, humanism, parenting, their process of shared decision-making, their unpretentious and nonmaterialistic lifestyle, their loyalty to one another—all essential elements of the rational and responsible life they had shared. In retirement they were virtually inseparable.

But now I was left wondering whether their self-conscious bond of shared values was quite enough. Had death dissolved their bond? Is death by itself so powerful that in ending a life it also, in a sense, cancels it? Or had there been another element—psychological, spiritual, or perhaps metaphysical—that came between them at the end to betray and darken the patient work of a lifetime?

FOR A FEW YEARS AFTER Dad's death, I had vivid recurrent dreams about him. In one kind of dream, he would be stricken with a life-threatening illness. I'd visit him in the hospital, interrogate the doctors and nurses about his diagnosis and treatment, and run after specialists and researchers in an attempt to discover some miracle cure.

In another kind of dream, I would try to dissuade him from taking his own life. Usually we would be having an oddly relaxed conversation, as if our life-and-death topic were mildly important but not earth-shaking, like who should be elected president, or the comparative merits of world religions. In this dream, he would patiently attend to my arguments, but in the end adhere to his belief that killing himself was the best course.

In another variation, I'd dream that I'd only dreamed that he was dead and wake up within my dream to find him still alive, though mortally ill.

In the fourth and rarest kind of dream, he had been transferred to another realm of existence. Now and then he would present himself like a ghost in certain familiar places as I went about my daily business, or I'd catch a glimpse of him in that other realm, ensconced in a chair, intently listening to classical music or to a droning lecture delivered in a voice that sounded muffled to my ear.

Then, as if a spigot had been shut off, my dreams of Dad abruptly stopped. I kept expecting him to return to my dreams, but he never did.

One day a couple of years later, Mom handed me a small album filled with photos of Dad from various epochs. Perhaps I accepted the gift a bit tentatively, almost indifferently, which elicited a surprisingly stern rebuke from Mom: "Dave, you hardly ever talk about Dad anymore! He loved you very, very much. You were his heart's core. It's not right that you should forget your father and go through life as if he had never existed!"

Mom's reprimand stung, leaving me speechless and sullen for a time, until it dawned on me what a universe of complex emotional energy must be underneath Mom's outburst.

AS THE YEARS WENT BY, my entire frame of reference regarding my family and my world underwent a momentous shift. I thought about Dad less and less—not as if he'd never existed, but because I'd filed my memories of him in a locked drawer.

And then slowly, over time, I realized that Dad was not where I thought he was.

IN THE MID-1990S, I was working as assistant director of a shelter for runaway homeless youth in Albany, New York. The director was a vibrant, courageous woman named Laurel Thatcher—vibrant because she was passionate in her concern for neglected youth; courageous because she often had to fight the system to get attention and services for her kids. Together we ran an ad hoc pseudo-family for a dozen or so "throwaway" teens—a sort of mom-and-pop operation. Laurel sometimes jokingly referred to me as "Dad," although I'd never been a father.

As a middle-class, middle-aged white guy working with urban youth, I represented a cultural disconnect for many of the kids who'd had negative experiences with adults who looked and talked like me. Figuring I needed to break the ice somehow, I tried humor.

One day Maria, a Latina, came into my office to talk about her case. Glancing up at my bulletin board, she noticed a picture of Linda (looking particularly beautiful) and inquired, "Is that your wife?"

"No," I deadpanned, "It's just a picture of her."

Maria's eyes lost focus for a moment. Then she gave me a cockeyed look. "Are you supposed to be my counselor?" she asked skeptically.

Around the lunch table I'd make stupid jokes, often dipping into my father's time-worn repertoire. The kids would groan and say, "Dave, that's corny!" Laurel would laugh uproariously and call me a nut. In this way she provided me with validation as I worked to make myself more approachable. For approachability, my mild, good-humored, self-deprecating father, who seemed able to get along with anyone, was my role model.

Often I'd be engaged one-on-one with a kid and suddenly realize that I was channeling Dad's voice and attitude—reasoning, wise, responsive but never reactive, gently persuasive, appealing to a child's innate wisdom. The nonreactive piece was especially helpful, since many of the kids had undergone traumas and grown up around adults who were unpredictable and highly reactive. Sometimes I'd adopt Dad's approach self-consciously. At other times I'd discover it working through me of its own accord, as if a part of Dad's nature had merged into mine.

AFTER THE UNABOMBER crisis I became a man on a mission, committed to putting a human face on my mentally ill brother and changing people's minds about the death penalty. Over a fifteen-year period, I traveled to thirty-nine states and gave more than a thousand public speeches in which I repeated my painful family story and explained why I thought capital punishment was a terrible mistake.

Looking back, I realize that Dad could never have done what I'd done. I think he lacked my faith that people were capable of overcoming their prejudices and negative reactions through reason and empathy. He also possessed less self-confidence (and less ego) than I did. Yet somehow he'd managed to instill more self-confidence in me than he himself had by consistently showing how much he appreciated the unique person I was, by honoring my good intentions even when I lacked the means to carry them out. Far from competing with his sons, he expected and wanted us to exceed him. Perhaps his innate spirit found a home in me, and a mode of actualization in my more assertive personality.

IF IT'S TRUE THAT DAD'S spirit lives on in me, then what am I to make of his suicide? Of the way he seemingly cut his loved ones off by cutting off his own future (however brief and painful that future might have been)? I cannot dismiss the resemblance between Ted's history of severing relationships and Dad's suicide, given that Dad never explained himself or said goodbye. Do I possess a similar capacity to cut myself off?

Honestly, I think the capacity is there, although mostly repressed. Perhaps it is expressed in my love for the desert, which offers a feeling of aloneness I treasure. A few years ago, on a visit to our land and cabin there, I went on a brief backpacking trip in a remote area of Big Bend National Park. On this trip I began writing a short story about a man on his deathbed.

Meanwhile, Linda and I had miscommunicated about the length of time I planned to be away, so when I failed to return on the day Linda expected, she became frightened. After the sun went down, she made a phone call to the park ranger's station to report a missing hiker, which unleashed a chain reaction among all the county's emergency rescue services: the National Park Service, the sheriff's department, even the U.S. Border Patrol.

As I trudged homeward the next morning, I knew something was amiss when I saw a helicopter circling above me. Before long, I found myself face-to-face with an expert Mexican American tracker who had been sent out to find me — or what was left of me.

Linda later told me that she had experienced an emotional crisis, assuming that I had died. For one long night, my assumed death became her new reality. In some sense, then, she has experienced my death. Who knows what parallel psychological truth we were sharing (or failing to share) during our three days apart, culminating in Linda's false belief that we were separated forever?

WHEN A LOVED ONE leaves us on purpose, it's only natural to speculate and imagine how we might have failed them. Often these speculations boil down to the realization that we lacked sufficient insight and empathy to appreciate the other person's suffering.

Last fall, when Linda and I buried my parents' ashes near our Texas cabin, we paused to say a few words over each of them. I felt deeply moved to apologize to them both. I knew I had some things to atone for, even if I had been a good son for the most part, yet I could only confess what occurred to me at that moment.

My apology to Mom arose from my having grown up in a sexist culture that devalued the intellectual and spiritual gifts of women. I should have respected her intelligence more, especially when I was an adolescent and a young man.

My apology to Dad focused on an incident that occurred shortly before I left Illinois to live in Texas. I'd come home one afternoon from my bus-driving shift and noticed something new on the redwood-stained fence surrounding our back patio: a small toy propeller spinning in the breeze. Obviously, someone had nailed it up there.

"Who put that silly propeller on the fence?" I demanded as I entered the house. I must have been tired and grumpy. I was also full of grandiose ideas in those days. The little propeller must have struck me as frivolous and lacking in dignity.

"Yes, it *is* a bit silly," Mom agreed. "Ted, why did you put the propeller on the fence?"

"I don't know," Dad said. "It was just an impulse."

Dad set his newspaper aside and went out and took the propeller down.

Years later at his graveside, I felt bad about stifling his light-hearted impulse. That little propeller twirling in the breeze now represents to me a lightness of spirit I wish I had the ability to recover.

< CHAPTER 4 >

NORTH STAR

WHEN WE MET IN THE seventh grade, I didn't pay much attention to this small, quiet girl named Linda. Somehow, despite her self-effacing manner, she was popular enough to be elected class vice president. That entitled her to select the records played at the school's Friday night dances, which I did not attend.

At the end of the school year, before final report cards were issued, our teacher, Mr. Fleming, announced that four students in his class had earned straight A's for the year. He invited these students to stand up as their names were called.

I wasn't at all surprised when I heard the teacher pronounce Linda's name. But I was stunned when I heard mine, since I had been slacking off in my studies.

I don't remember the names of the other straight-A students. I do remember standing there in the sterile classroom on a cloudy afternoon, the day's boredom suddenly inflected with surprise. Maybe Mr. Fleming saw something in me that didn't register on mundane exams.

Linda and I stood one row apart near the back of the classroom. It was my first hint of a connection between us beyond sharing space in Mr. Fleming's "accelerated" seventh-grade class.

The following year, in eighth grade, I sensed Linda shyly reaching out to me on a few occasions. Thanks to those Friday night dances that I didn't attend, she now had a boyfriend, who happened to be my buddy Keith. Keith's mother and mine were friends. Keith and I also had the same birthday. Otherwise we were as different as can be. Keith was extraverted, always bubbling over with emotions. I was even-tempered and reserved, almost dogmatically rational in my approach to most topics.

One day after school I attended a basketball game in the school gym. Linda and Keith entered a bit late. Linda led Keith along the row of bleachers where I was sitting and plunked herself down next to me. After a while I noticed her toying with one of her shoes. Since I didn't have any sisters and since I had very little experience with girls, I assumed that this was something girls ordinarily did.

A few minutes later she turned to me and whispered: "I lost my shoe. Can you help me find it?"

The next thing I knew, we were poking around together in the dim, somewhat private space under the bleachers. Linda's shoe wasn't difficult to find. I'm not sure we ever directly looked at each other, surely not face-to-face or gazing into one another's eyes. Kissing? Forget it. I was much too reserved for that. Perhaps it was merely the circumstance of being alone with a girl for the first time in my life at the onset of puberty, but I was overwhelmed by an unaccustomed feeling—not attraction per se, but rather a strong sense of having known this person, possibly for a long time, in another context. It wasn't déjà vu, since there was nothing about the place, the sounds, or the light that felt uncannily familiar, only Linda herself.

Keith showed up under the bleachers a little later. He looked puzzled. That strange feeling left me as suddenly as it had come. Once again we were just three kids thrown together in an innocent play—a shining adolescent girl with two foggy-headed boys.

The event produced no real change inside me. I didn't from that day spend a lot of time and emotional energy thinking about Linda. My eyes weren't constantly drawn to her. During freshman year of high school, for example, I hardly remember seeing her. During our sophomore and junior years, however, we were again thrown together in advanced science classes.

I was aware that Linda had picked a seat close to mine in sophomore physics class. Before the bell rang, she sometimes talked to me about her smart older brother who was majoring in mathematics at the University of Chicago and played in a jazz band. She must have known that I, too, had a smart older brother who studied math.

Evergreen Park, Illinois, was a lower-middle-class, white enclave where the standard aspiration was economic rather than intellectual. Even kids who weren't especially bright intended to go to college to obtain a ticket to success that their parents never had. The town's official nickname was "The Village of Churches," meaning, I guess, that spiritual aspirations were more or less standardized as well. But I had even less exposure to the churches than I did to girls.

I'd come to think of myself as somewhat above the crowd, harboring dreams that were more important than the conventional aspirations of my classmates. In the way she talked about her brother, Linda signaled that she, too, was casting her eyes on wider horizons.

In our junior advanced chemistry class, Linda chose me as her lab partner. That's when the chemistry of our friendship began. Conducting experiments together—handling the vials, tubes, chemicals, and little measuring spoons; carefully observing and documenting the results—was a mostly wordless business that bred feelings of cooperation and intimacy between us. Those same feelings extended to our whispered small talk after the experiments were done.

In these conversations, I learned about Linda's sense of connection with animals, both wild and domestic. She spoke about Tasha and Calypso, her dog and cat, as if they were family members. Since I'd grown up in a household without pets other than Teddy's parakeet, Linda's affection for animals struck me as exotic.

I spent a couple of weeks working up my courage to invite my new lab partner to the class prom, until one day I overheard a couple of kids talking:

"Oh, Linda? Yeah, she's going steady with Kenny. I think she really loves him. At least it looks that way."

Kenny was a hunky athlete — the most talented in our town — and a charter member of the school's in-crowd. He was also a nice guy with a very modest demeanor, kind to everyone regardless of social status. I'd been his teammate on the Little League All-Star team. I had liked Kenny without feeling I had much in common with him.

However, I did a double take when I learned that Linda was dating Kenny, since Kenny and I were so different. Imagining that Linda might see something special in me, I was left wondering what in the world she saw in Kenny.

Inevitably I would encounter Linda and Kenny walking hand in hand, boyfriend and girlfriend, in the hallways of the school. I would nod a formal hello. When Linda said hello back, our eyes often met in a shared glance that went straight to my heart. Everyone else, including Kenny, was cast in shadow by that glance — mere phantoms surrounding two human beings who existed especially for each other. Was I imagining this? Did Linda greet others with a glance that conveyed similar recognition? All I knew was that no one had ever looked at me so intimately, with eyes that both touched me and saw me truly.

A year later our family moved to a small town in Iowa. I was lonely there, feeling uprooted from my past and alienated from the small-town community where I'd been dropped. Now and then I helped out at the small factory my father ran. An older coworker asked me one day: "Have you found a girlfriend yet?" "No," I said. "Hey, you're behind the times," he rejoined.

I'd been behind the times all my life.

One evening, as I lay in bed on a still night, I was entranced by moonlight casting shadows on the ancient patterned wallpaper of my new bedroom. Gazing at those shadows, I experienced a moment of sudden illumination.

"I love Linda," I told myself. "I'll love her forever. There's no going back on that."

The words welled up out of my loneliness, and I suspect from some deeper place as well.

Two days later, I wrote her a letter.

THE NEXT YEAR, WHILE attending colleges far apart, Linda and I exchanged torrid letters. Released from the social fetters of our hometown, we were finally free to love one another—or so I thought. I imagined that at the end of the school year we might hop in my old Chevy, drive westward into mythical landscapes, and leave all those dusty books and conventional reality behind.

However, Linda had found herself a boyfriend at her college. This was to become a recurrent theme. My dream of unfettered love fizzled.

After college, just as it appeared that the force of gravity was pulling us back together again, Linda met and married a fellow graduate student. I was crushed. I meditated on the question *Can I go through life loving a woman who doesn't love me back?*

The answer that came to me was not necessarily the one I wanted: *Yes.*

My infatuation with Linda is not too difficult to understand. She was and is beautiful, highly intelligent, and spiritually sensitive. She had also reached out to me in ways that no other girl had ever done. Romantic love was a theme that permeated the popular culture of the 1950s and early 1960s. As an idealist, I was prone to idealizing the first girl who got ahold of my heartstrings. I even concocted a quasi-rational argument to support my fixation: *Affection that depends on a reciprocal return of affection is not so much love as it is a form of commerce.* I convinced myself that unrequited love was love in its purest form, akin to the love of God, a spiritualization of the human possibility of love transcending objectification. (Once you're invested in this way of approaching love and spirituality, there may be no way of going back without becoming ridiculous.)

But there is another side to the love equation as well. Does it matter whether God is really *there?* The mystery of the meaning of *there* appears to be where God "lives," both inside and outside ourselves. Similarly, Linda was always *there* for me—a real person existing beyond my fantasies, someone my deepest intuitions could somehow "touch," a presence in my universe that confirmed itself in various ways: when we met, when I thought about her, as someone simply and always *there.*

A Tibetan Buddhist monk once summed up our connection in another way, moving his hands together as if to gently compress a package. "Very strong karma!" he commented.

AT THE AGE OF thirty-three, with nothing much to hold me back— no satisfying work, no prospects with Linda, my life stalled, seeing the world's technological culture as fatally contaminated by nihilism—I decided to make the journey beyond conventional reality on my own.

I wandered into the West Texas wilderness, where I spent the next eight years living as a desert hermit. Every day, at least once, I spoke Linda's name under my breath like a secret mantra.

Years later, after we had married, I asked a therapist whether my infatuation with Linda had been psychologically unhealthy. She said that it *would* have been unhealthy if Linda had not *eventually* reciprocated my love.

Once we began living together, our relationship felt entirely natural, as if preordained. I felt I'd never known what happiness was before.

I asked Linda why it had taken her so long to fall in love with me.

She answered flippantly: "Dave, you always had a bad haircut."

In a more serious tone, she said I'd never really told her how I felt about her.

I found that impossible to believe. "Linda," I argued, "in all those letters we exchanged, I told you over and over again that I loved you."

"No, you didn't," she insisted. "And I can prove it!"

It was then I learned that Linda had saved every single one of my letters going back more than twenty years, just as I had saved all of hers. Together we pored over my letters — scores and scores of them. They were riddled with artistic pretentions and sophomoric speculations, but nowhere could I find the telling, straightforward phrase "I love you."

"I told you so!" she said.

"Smart as you are," I replied, "you should have been able to read between the lines."

"Smart as you are," she rejoined, "you should have known what a woman needs to hear!"

AT ITS PEAK, THE FEDERAL government's hunt for the Unabomber involved 125 agents working full time. Millions of dollars were poured into the investigation. In the end, the case was cracked by Linda, a private citizen unconnected to the massive investigation. She had never met the person responsible for sending the bombs, only his family.

On September 19, 1995, about a month after Linda had first broached her suspicions to me and six years after we had begun living together, the Unabomber's manifesto was published in the *Washington Post*. I read a news story about it in my local newspaper and felt vindicated. The manifesto was said to propound "neoconservative" views. Although Ted had sometimes considered our parents' liberal philosophy naive, I'd never thought of him as politically conservative.

To the best of my knowledge, he was apolitical. Whatever "neoconservativism" was, I couldn't imagine that label fitting my brother.

Publication of the manifesto allowed me to fulfill my promise to Linda to compare it with my brother's ideas and writing. She made a phone call to our local newspaper to find out where the *Washington Post* was sold, then dispatched me to a newsstand, one of the few in our area that carried the *Post*.

By the time I arrived, however, the last of six copies had been sold.

As a lifelong baseball fan, I soon became engrossed in following the World Series. A subsequent visit from Mom further diverted our attention through Columbus Day.

It was not until the following Saturday, after breakfast at a local diner, that Linda suggested we go to the library to find a copy of the September 19 *Washington Post* containing the manifesto.

We found that the Schenectady County Public Library had not yet received its copy through the mail. I was willing to wait, but Linda was less patient. "Let's try the Union College library!" she said. I sighed and tagged along.

At Union, we soon located the September 19 issue but were disappointed to discover that the special insert containing the manifesto had been removed. "Obviously," I thought, "we're not meant to read this thing today."

But Linda persisted. "The Internet!" she exclaimed. "It's probably posted on the Internet by now."

What an irony, I thought, that I should be using the hypermodern Internet to find out whether my technophobic brother is an antitechnology terrorist. The very thought gave me a slightly queasy feeling.

Soon I found myself in front of a computer screen at the Union College library. It was my first time on the Internet. As I began to read the manifesto, I became aware that Linda wasn't looking at the computer screen. She was gazing at my face. Since she'd never met Ted, she knew that my face would tell her more than the words on the screen.

I fully expected to be able to turn to Linda and say, "It's definitely not him! Now do you see how silly you've been?"

But as I finished the first paragraph, I sat immobilized, my eyes glued to the screen. I read on. I remember feeling a slight rush of adrenaline. My emotions were a mixture of fear, dismay, anger. I'd sometimes reacted this way while reading one of Ted's hurtful letters.

In the opening lines of the manifesto, I detected a tone similar to Ted's when he wrote letters condemning our parents. Only here the indictment was vastly expanded. On the surface, the phraseology was calm and intellectual, but it barely concealed the author's smoldering rage. As much as I wanted to, I couldn't turn to Linda and honestly say that the writing was not my brother's.

That day we were able to retrieve only the first six pages of the manifesto. After the first page or two, the manuscript abruptly veered away from its opening theme and embarked on a puzzling critique of the political Left. Apparently this was the section that had earned the "neoconservative" label.

The public space at Union College Library was not an appropriate place to discuss whether my brother Ted had authored the Unabomber's manifesto. But as soon as we stepped outside Linda questioned me in an anxious whisper: "What do you think? Do you think he wrote it?"

"I'll be honest with you. Some parts of it *do* sound like him," I murmured, bending my head toward hers. "But other parts don't sound familiar at all. I don't know what to think. If I *had* to estimate, I'd say there's maybe one chance in a thousand that Ted might have written it."

As we walked back toward the parking lot, Linda was very quiet. Finally she said, "David, one chance in a thousand that your brother is a serial killer? Maybe we need to do something."

I had no answer for her. In my heart I recognized that her fears could no longer be dismissed.

I didn't know much about the Unabomber case. I hadn't followed it in the news. I don't remember even hearing the word "Unabomber" prior to December 1994, when I read reports of a mail bomb that had claimed the life of Thomas Mosser, an advertising executive in New Jersey. Only later did I learn that the Unabomber saga had served as regular grist for crime-oriented television programs like *America's Most Wanted*. Linda and I didn't watch much television.

Surely, I thought, there must be old newspaper and magazine articles filled with details and clues. Perhaps if I read those articles, I'd find some piece of information that would put our fears to rest.

I dropped Linda off at home—she had a ton of papers to grade—and immediately drove back to the Schenectady County Public Library to conduct some research. I pulled out the *Reader's Guide* and found a couple of dozen entries under "Unabomber," several of which I located in the library's periodicals archive. For the first time, I read detailed accounts of the attacks, including the names of the victims, their pictures, a summary of their professional careers, the comments of their coworkers and devastated family members, the circumstances surrounding the explosions, and the speculations of law enforcement officials.

I studied the police sketch of the presumed Unabomber based on a woman's recollection of a man she'd glimpsed minutes before a bomb went off in Salt Lake City in 1987. I gazed at the drawing long and carefully. It depicted a youngish, mustachioed male in a hooded sweatshirt with aviator sunglasses. To my mind, it didn't particularly resemble Ted.

Accompanying the sketch was a physical description, also based on the eyewitness's sighting. It described someone three inches taller than Ted and ten years younger, with hair that was light, not dark brown like Ted's. Reading this, I felt relieved. With three points of difference, the description didn't match my brother, so he probably wasn't the Unabomber after all.

From the articles I gleaned other encouraging bits of information. For instance, forensic profilers backed up the witness's impression that the Unabomber was about ten years younger than Ted. From the writing, they deduced an author without an advanced degree, whereas Ted held a PhD from the University of Michigan. They speculated that the Unabomber might have worked for an airline or in some blue-collar field. Ted was a former college professor.

But no matter how hard I hunted for a piece of information that would eliminate Ted as a suspect, I never found it. As far as I knew, he'd spent years and years in his cabin continuously. He hated to travel and seldom did so. He lived a primitive life without money more than a thousand miles from northern California, where most of the bombs had been placed or mailed. He had taught himself how to survive in the wilderness. He had learned to read and write Spanish fluently. He still dabbled in mathematics. He'd written frequent, long letters to his family—until one day the letters abruptly stopped.

Had my brilliant, intense brother occupied himself with destructive projects we knew nothing about?

I carefully reviewed the timeline of the bombings. Nothing jumped out at me except the date of the very first bomb, which exploded on the Chicago campus of the University of Illinois in May 1978. In the summer of 1978, Ted made one of his rare trips home to earn some money. In fact, Ted, our father, and I worked at the same factory for a while. But I was positive that Ted had arrived by bus in *late June* of 1978. He'd even telephoned en route to let us know his scheduled time of arrival. He told us he was calling from a bus station in Minnesota or someplace. So barring an elaborate plan of deception—including lodging himself for a month somewhere in the Chicago area without his family's knowledge—Ted must have been in Montana in May 1978, so he could not have placed that first bomb. It never occurred to me that Ted could be deceptive.

I hurried home and reported the good news to Linda: the physical description didn't match Ted, the victims had no discernible connection to him, and I'd discovered nothing to implicate my brother in any of the bombings.

But if I thought any of this would make a difference to Linda, I was mistaken. She did not seem to feel relieved. No matter where the facts seemed to be pointing, Linda had a strong intuition that my brother was the Unabomber.

If Linda had been more easily convinced of Ted's innocence, I might not have felt any reason to say what I said next: "You know, hon, there's just one thing that troubles me: that sketch from Salt Lake City. I never knew until today that there had been a bombing in Salt Lake City. I do remember that Ted once had a job working construction in Salt Lake City. In fact, I visited him there. It was a long time ago. But . . ."

While doing nothing wasn't an option, the options we did face were not very appealing. Should we notify the FBI? In my view, that could prove disastrous. I reminded Linda of the FBI's ill-advised attempts to make arrests at Waco and Ruby Ridge, which resulted in many deaths. I reminded her of Ted's paranoia and emotional fragility. What evidence did we really have against Ted? Why would the FBI take us seriously? And if they did, what if their investigation turned belligerent?

Suppose they sent an agent to his cabin to ask questions. In Ted's paranoid state, he might panic and react badly, even if he were completely innocent. If he found out that I'd reported him, he would deeply resent my suspicion or think I'd behaved maliciously, and this would foreclose any possibility of reconciliation between us. In the worst case, he might lash out at an agent: fear does strange things to people. Or he might hurt himself, convinced that the peace of mind he so desperately craved was unavailable, even in the wilderness.

No matter what happened, the effect on Ted was bound to be disturbing—and to judge by his letters, he was pretty disturbed already.

Linda and I settled on a quieter approach, more suited to our experiences and instincts. We both felt at home in a world of ideas and words. We knew how to make books open up to us and reveal the minds of their authors. Perhaps, we reasoned, if we read the Unabomber's manifesto several times very carefully, we could discover the truth. Besides, I had dozens and dozens of Ted's old letters tucked away in a trunk in the attic. Some of those letters touched on the theme of technology. By carefully comparing Ted's letters to the manifesto, we could possibly discern whether Ted had written both.

I told Linda that I had two good reasons to believe my brother was not the Unabomber. First, he had never been violent. People in their midthirties don't just wake up some day and decide to start hurting people. Antisocial types usually start causing harm at a much earlier age.

Second, the Unabomber's rant against political leftism, prominently placed near the beginning of the manifesto, wasn't consistent with Ted's main concern about technology, nor had I heard him voice any similar views in the past. The author of the manifesto wanted to fend off any notion that a political solution could be effective against the threat posed by technology. His thesis was more radical: he argued that the problem lay much deeper than politics could plausibly reach.

Ted had also been a young professor at Berkeley, a hotbed of radicalism during the '60s, a time of social and political turmoil. Ted's alienation from "the alienated generation" recalled Bob Dylan's line "He was always on the outside of whatever side there was." So I wouldn't have expected Ted to get cozy with left-wing environmentalists.

But even if Ted believed exactly what the Unabomber had written, I wouldn't have thought he'd write something with the energy or tone of the manifesto's attack on leftism, which appeared to emanate from a place of deep personal disappointment. Could it be that our parent's liberal politics (our father, to vex his friends, would occasionally claim to be a pacifist and a socialist; and Mom, against the grain of 1950s McCarthyism, sympathized with communism in theory if not as practiced) had generated something more than a dismissive reaction in my older brother? If so, why hadn't I heard about it before?

Over the next three or four weeks, Linda and I fell into a routine. The Unabomber (whoever he was) had promised to stop killing if his writings were published. We hoped the manifesto's publication would at least buy us time as the shadowy killer absorbed the public's reaction to his treatise.

Every evening after work, Linda and I would come home, eat dinner, and retire to a couch in our living room. There, instead of reading books or watching television or talking about the day's events like most couples, we'd sit side by side poring over the manifesto and piles of my brother's old letters.

Linda relied in large measure on my familiarity with my brother's views and personality. On the other hand, she couldn't possibly trust my objectivity. It was as if two people were looking at a body of water from different angles. From her position on shore, Linda could only see the surface of the water. Hovering above, I could see to the bottom of the lake, understand the psychological struggles beneath the surface of my brother's ideas and arguments. At times I thought I vaguely glimpsed in those depths a vision of my brother as the traumatized baby our mother had once described, eyes crossed in terror, strapped to a hospital gurney, stripped of all security and trust.

Linda and I endlessly discussed our readings of the manifesto and of Ted's letters. As with any interpretation, we were constantly left wondering how much of what we saw was our own projection and how much was an authentic reflection of the author, whether the author was my brother or someone else.

Occasionally I'd look up from my task and reflect on how bizarre it all felt. *Am I really doing this?*

We never found the proverbial smoking gun. I identified one phrase that gave me pause: the author of the manifesto suggested that modern philosophers were not living up to their reputation as "cool-headed logicians."

I felt sure that Ted had once used the same peculiar phrase in a letter, but I couldn't find the letter. Of course, I didn't have all his letters at hand. Some were at Mom's house in Chicago and others were stored away in my Texas cabin. A few had been lost over the years.

Each day felt different as the pendulum of belief swung between one kind of doubt and its opposite. One day I'd read the manifesto and could almost hear my brother's voice speaking each word. I'd say to myself: *The truth is staring you in the face, only you refuse to see it.*

The very next day I'd reason with myself: *Linda has planted a suspicion in your mind. You've been worried about your brother. Our fear is built on worry and projection, nothing more.*

I had some powerful dreams during this period. In one memorable dream, Linda and I were together in a farm field, bending down over some manual work, planting or picking or weeding. At one point Linda glanced up and exclaimed, "Hey Dave, look at that!" She then pointed to some threatening storm clouds boiling darkly on the horizon. "Maybe they're coming our way. Maybe we should warn the neighbors," she urged. "No, there's nothing we can do," I said, and resumed my work. But Linda was insistent, which greatly irritated me. "It's got nothing to do with us!" I shouted. "Forget it!"

One Saturday morning, I awoke with a crushing sense of depression. I made my way to the kitchen table and sat down. I found Linda, who had gotten up earlier, munching on cornflakes. I caught her eye. My words spilled out unplanned: "Hon, I think there might be a fifty-fifty chance that Ted wrote the manifesto."

Linda knew what it cost me to say those words. Now what were we going to do? Continue thinking and talking and procrastinating while perhaps my brother was constructing another bomb?

For the rest of that day we wrestled with it. I say "it" because the word Unabomber was too frightening to say out loud. Linda sometimes shortened it to "UB," but instead I grasped instinctively at the neutral, impersonal pronoun.

Was Ted the UB or wasn't he? Should we do something? Should we talk to Mom? How long would the Unabomber wait before he struck again?

You might think these questions represented a logical sequence, but in reality they came at us from all directions at once.

I felt that reacting impulsively to our fears could result in great harm. However, Linda pointed out that waiting too long might also allow great harm to occur. We talked about it all day long, but by nightfall we felt even more confused and upset. We decided to sleep on it. Perhaps we'd wake up in the morning and the answer would be there.

But sleep eluded us. As we lay awake side by side, I talked about how troubled I felt, wondering if I'd ever really known my brother. If Ted were the Unabomber, he was responsible for wanton, cruel attacks on innocent strangers — for evil stuff.

I realized that my feelings toward my brother had subtly shifted. I'd never considered Ted capable of violence. In fact, my only fear along those lines was the haunting worry that he might someday kill himself.

I reminded myself of the cruel letters that Ted had written to Mom and Dad — emotional bombs, you might call them. But I always saw those letters as cries of pain. I couldn't uncover any memories that revealed deep-seated evil in my brother. In fact, the memories that flooded in were mostly fond ones.

I told Linda how Teddy had tried to give me his most prized possession — a coin collection — when I returned home from a brief stay in the hospital. "Teddy, your brother knows how you feel about him," I remembered Mom saying. "You don't need to give Davy your coin collection. He knows you love him."

Among the college philosophy courses Linda had taught over the years were courses in ethics. As a youth counselor at Equinox Youth Shelter, I was acutely aware of the dilemmas that teenagers sometimes face. I always counseled the kids against violence, even in violent circumstances. Many had come to distrust adults, particularly adults in positions of authority. I always urged them to find some adult to confide in when it was a matter of protecting someone's health or safety. But now I realized how easy it had been to lecture the kids — to urge them, "Do the right thing!" — when the risks and costs would be borne by them, not me.

I had to ask myself, *What if we turn Ted in and he's convicted and eventually executed? What would it be like to go through the rest of my life with my brother's blood on my hands?*

The impact on Ted would be devastating. The impact on me would be devastating. Turning in my brother would have to be a considered act, not a thoughtless one. The damage to my brother could not be undone.

I also had to think about the effect all this would have on Mom. She was a seventy-nine-year-old widow. For years she had worried about Ted because of his emotional problems, his isolation, and his estrangement from the family. But I knew her worst fear about Ted didn't even come close to the awful suspicion that Linda and I were struggling with: that he might be a serial killer.

Mom would be crushed. She might even die of a stroke or heart failure. I couldn't imagine how I could begin to comfort her. Her wounds would never, ever heal. I couldn't be sure our relationship would survive.

I wasn't really thinking about justice. All I wanted was to minimize harm to everyone. The past — already overflowing with tragedy and suffering — could not be undone. Now it seemed that we could act to save lives only by sacrificing the life of my mentally ill brother.

There was no simple ethical formula that could make our decision less agonizing, no way of knowing we wouldn't come to regret our decision in the future. But no one else could stop Ted if he really was the Unabomber.

Linda made one other argument to push me toward our terrible choice. It was an argument formulated by Socrates in Plato's *Gorgias* dialogue. According to Socrates, treating others unjustly causes harm to the perpetrator as well as to the victim of injustice. It would be an act of cruelty to permit your worst enemy to behave unjustly: for example, to let him get away with murder. Linda argued that allowing Ted to continue hurting others would only result in greater damage to Ted—harsher punishment in the long run, psychological distress, spiritual deterioration, greater madness. Her Buddhist analysis arrived at the same conclusion, only more so, given the doctrine of rebirth. Through his acts of violence Ted was accumulating negative karma that could cause him immense future suffering.

These intellectual arguments reached across a moral abyss, but the bridge they formed was tenuous. I wasn't sure it would hold up under the weight of reality—especially if Ted got the death penalty. I countered that Ted might be innocent. Pointing the authorities to an innocent man—especially one with paranoid tendencies—could lead to disaster.

I needed something more to go on than guesswork and intuition. I told Linda I needed to visit Ted at his cabin in Montana.

This suggestion upset Linda.

"It's not to confront him," I tried to reassure her. "I won't even mention the Unabomber. I just know that if I see him and spend some time with him, I'll learn something."

"But David," Linda countered. "He might hurt you. He's got guns, doesn't he? I can't let you go out there!"

"Hon, I'm sure Ted would never hurt me."

"David, a month ago you didn't believe he was capable of hurting anyone. The truth of the matter is that we really *don't know* what he's capable of!"

After going back and forth for a while, we hit on a compromise: I'd write to Ted, ask for permission to visit, and wait for his response. Linda and I could make a decision once we heard back from him. Maybe Linda was counting on Ted to discourage me, since I hadn't received a friendly letter from him in years.

In the letter I wrote, I told Ted I missed him. I said I had some vacation time coming and would be happy to drive him to Helena to pick up supplies before the heavy snows came. I tried to invest all the love and concern I felt for Ted in a simple and straightforward letter. There was no way I could put my heart on the page, but I hoped Ted might somehow feel it and understand.

Ted's reply came two weeks later. I was alone at home after work when I retrieved his letter from our mail slot. I sat down on the living room couch and gazed at the envelope for a minute. My name and address were handprinted in the familiar block letters I'd seen on every letter Ted had sent me since college. I noticed my hand trembling slightly as I held the envelope.

My heart sank as I read the opening lines:

> I get just choked with frustration at my inability to get our stinking family off my back once and for all, and "stinking family" emphatically includes you. I DON'T EVER WANT TO SEE YOU OR HEAR FROM YOU, OR ANY OTHER MEMBER OF OUR FAMILY, AGAIN.

The letter was a short one for Ted: two sides of one sheet of notebook paper. Ted's anger and coldness were truly incomprehensible to me. I couldn't fathom what was going on inside his mind.

"He's gone over the edge," I murmured.

I realized I couldn't reason with him; I couldn't control him. And now it struck me that he probably could not control himself either.

BY THIS TIME THE Thanksgiving holiday was fast upon us. Linda and I were planning to make the drive to Chicago to visit both of our families. I intended to recover several of Ted's letters that I'd left in a dresser drawer of my old bedroom at Mom's house. If a postmark definitively placed Ted in Montana on the same date the Unabomber had placed or mailed one of his bombs a thousand miles away in California, then we could rule him out.

Meanwhile, Linda and I both agreed it was time to bring Mom closer to us. We didn't want her to be far away if the worst happened.

So after Thanksgiving dinner we sat her down and made our case. The old house was becoming too much for her to handle, we pointed out. She should be closer to family in case she got sick again. It would be nice to see her more often.

Mom said she would think about it and let us know. She had some good friends she'd hate to leave behind. Overall, the visit wasn't a joyful one. Later that evening, she took me to task for not caring as much as I should about my brother. Had Mom intuitively channeled the secret deliberations that Linda and I were engaged in? It certainly felt that way.

None of the postmarks on Ted's letters provided the kind of alibi I was hoping for. The conflict between our moral obligation and my love for my brother could not be reconciled. We could not act, or fail to act, without sacrificing one for the other. Perhaps we would wake up some day and see our situation differently. Perhaps our sacrifice — illuminated by reason and necessity — would feel less painful over time. But if we waited for some magical resolution of our dilemma, we could end up waiting forever. We could end up waiting until someone else got killed.

I was too consumed with my own confusion and helplessness to appreciate the difficulty of Linda's position. Not only did it fall to her to push and plan and steer our investigation; she also had to motivate and comfort her reluctant partner along the difficult path.

After we returned to New York, I asked Linda for two weeks of silence on our all-consuming topic. I needed to go inward, to my spiritual core if such a thing existed, in hopes of finding an answer I could live with. Linda granted me the two weeks and faithfully respected my process throughout that time. But no answer ever came to me.

I did have one very disturbing dream in which our familiar living room was gradually becoming smaller. Day by day I could detect no difference, no movement. But over time it grew clear that the room was much smaller than it had been. In fact, the furniture was beginning to crowd together. "Linda," I said, "we'd better get out of here before we're crushed!" Linda quickly understood what was going on. But then I noticed for the first time that the doorways had vanished. The walls were coming together and we were left with no escape.

One night shortly after the end of my two-week reprieve, Linda and I were lying awake in bed when I shared with her a warm memory of my last visit with Ted in 1986. During this visit, I'd been using a couple of sawhorses to cut up some limbs for firewood when I suddenly lost my balance and fell roughly to the ground. I heard Ted running up.

"I hope I didn't break your saw," I offered. I knew that my brother only had a few tools and that he treated them with great care.

"I don't care anything about the saw!" my brother exclaimed. "Are you OK?"

My voice trailed off as I finished recounting this incident. Then the stillness of our bedroom was abruptly broken by Linda's sobs. I hugged her, trying to comfort her, but soon I, too, was crying uncontrollably. For a long time, we clutched each other tightly in the darkness.

When the crying was over, we lay there quietly. A discernible shift had taken place. The tangled brush of argument, speculation, and doubt had been swept away by this surge of pent-up emotions.

"We have to do something," Linda said.

I knew she was right.

WHATEVER WAS GOING to happen—all the unpredictable consequences that might follow from our actions—lay beyond our control. Try as we might to minimize the harm to Ted, Mom, and anyone else who might be affected, we could fail. But we shared one overriding concern: to prevent the Unabomber from claiming more victims.

Christmas came and went. Linda and I drove the wintry roads back to Chicago to visit our families. Over Christmas dinner, Mom told us she had thought about moving to New York and had reached a decision. With sudden cheerfulness, she announced that she had decided to sell the old house and move to an apartment close to us. It meant saying goodbye to her friends, letting go of some of the past, and embracing a new and different future closer to her son and daughter-in-law.

We went into the living room to open Christmas presents. As the evening wore on and we sat among the fresh gifts and crumpled wrapping paper, Mom said, "I hope Ted is not feeling sad today. Oh, I hope he doesn't feel lonely thinking about the Christmases we used to have. Maybe he has some friend who invited him over today so he's not all alone."

At this point Linda got up and went to the bathroom.

"I hope so too," I said with little optimism.

"Dad and I always used to say our happiest times were when you boys were young. We looked back on those times with such fondness. We had such good times, didn't we? Do you remember those happy times, David? Were they happy times for you?"

"Of course, Mom. Those were wonderful times. I'll never forget them."

I changed the subject, wanting to talk about the future instead of the past. After awhile I realized that Linda had been in the bathroom for a long time. I got up to check on her. I knocked on the door but got no answer. When I turned the doorknob and entered Mom's pitifully small bathroom, I nearly bumped into Linda, who was sitting on the toilet lid, tears streaming down her face.

I ALWAYS COME BACK to what, for me, represents a deep mystery: what kind of intuitive leap enabled Linda to solve a crime that had baffled a generation of skilled investigators, allowed her to identify a suspect whose close family members believed him incapable of such violence?

I imagine she pieced together the truth in the same way that people generally do: by fitting fragments together to constitute a larger picture. Still, she discovered, in my view, a truth that was greater than the sum of its parts. As a fly on the wall during many family discussions aimed at understanding Ted and brainstorming how we might help him, she picked up on elements that escaped us. Whereas our family conversations were mainly self-referential—*What did we do wrong? How can we help our son/brother?*—Linda, as a sensitive outsider, saw clearly what we couldn't: that Ted was beyond any help his family could give him. Intuitively, she *felt* his capacity for violence. By witnessing his parents' agony, sorrow, and confusion she realized quite clearly that the damage caused by raw emotional violence is of a piece with the damage caused by physical violence. If Ted was capable of wounding his parents so deeply, then he was capable of almost anything.

Looking back on our journey as a couple through the ethical dilemma we faced and its aftermath, I see more clearly something I couldn't fully appreciate at the time: we took that terrible journey both together and apart, deeply bonded in some ways and quite alone and isolated in others.

Linda led the way and discovered the only way out of our small hell, which was through compassion for those whom Ted had hurt and those whom he might yet hurt.

But if I had not followed her, Linda probably would have gotten nowhere. Very likely there would have been more victims. Very likely, too, the integrity, the very essence of our love for one another would have been compromised, and our marriage might not have survived.

Looking back, it all seems like a strange dream. Had it felt more real, I don't know how we could have survived with our sanity intact. While I am still dreaming that dream, writing this memoir, delivering lectures now and then on mental illness or the death penalty, writing occasional letters to my brother that I expect will go unanswered, needing to make sense of it all, Linda, I realize, would prefer to let the dream go, to live more fully in the moment, to recover the joy and newness we experienced in those first years of our marriage, before the Unabomber's shadow engulfed us.

I know that Linda, as usual, is right. She has paid plenty. Perhaps there is still time for us to share brighter dreams.

AFTERWORD

JAMES L. KNOLL IV, MD

LYING ON MY ANALYST'S COUCH, I was neurotic and complaining. It was 1998 and I was in the last year of my psychiatry residency. My neurosis was surging because I had recently been offered the opportunity for advanced training in forensic psychiatry by an intimidating living legend in the field: Phillip J. Resnick, MD. Resnick's forensic psychiatry training program was renowned for its rigor, intensity, and ego-annihilating tests of one's abilities. I knew that entering into the world of a forensic expert whose list of cases reads like a highlight reel of American criminal justice would irrevocably alter my life.[1] It was one of those rare moments that one is aware of standing on the precipice of a major life change.

At the time of my analytic kvetching, Dr. Resnick was hard at work examining innumerable boxes of records and journals of a man known to most only as the Unabomber. Resnick had been retained by prosecutors who were anticipating that Ted Kaczynski would raise a mental health defense. What may not have been anticipated was the strength of Ted Kaczynski's commitment to his ideals and his abhorrence to being labeled mentally ill. So strong was this opposition that he preferred the death penalty over allowing his defense attorneys to present mental health evidence.[2] Not only did he not believe he was mentally ill; more importantly, he did not want his philosophical ideals and opinions to be compromised or dismissed as the product of an unsound mind. After much difficult deliberation by the judge, attorneys, and Ted Kaczynski, the trial was preempted by a guilty plea that allowed him to avoid the death penalty.

My apprenticeship with Dr. Resnick began as he was wrapping up his work on the Unabomber case. Certainly I had heard of Ted Kaczynski already through the media, but I would come to learn much more about him during my time with Dr. Resnick. His teachings and commentary on the Unabomber case were factual and nonjudgmental and sought to truly understand him through a humanistic, albeit forensic psychiatric, lens. In addition to the forensic and psychiatric nuances, Resnick keenly perceived Ted Kaczynski's inner desire for an emotional connection and a meaningful intimate relationship. It was this last point that stuck with me. It was simply a fact per the forensic data, and ultimately it burrowed into my psyche. I was left with an enhanced understanding of the poignancy of the human need for attachment, regardless of the choices we make and the harm we cause each other.

Attachment as a complex concept used by mental health professionals should be distinguished from its connotation in Buddhism. Buddhist psychology has begun to influence Western approaches to mental health in the form of mindfulness therapy. However, Buddhism is a 2,500-year-old tradition that has been famously described as coming to the West via the science of psychology.[3] In the Buddhist tradition, attachment (synonymous with desire, greed, craving, envy) is considered one of the "three poisons" — along with aversion (hatred, anger) and ignorance (distraction, self-deception, delusion).

From the time *Homo sapiens* first developed conscious self-awareness, "these primal motives have been at the root of all misery."[4] Indeed, they are at work not only in individual minds, but also as ideologies motivating larger social systems.[5] The three poisons may be more clearly understood and then transcended through meditation, psychotherapy, and other compassionate mind-training techniques.

In a psychological context, *attachment theory* focuses on the dynamics of interpersonal relationships and on how we are profoundly influenced by caregivers during infancy. In this sense, attachment is not only a good thing, but crucial to one's social and emotional development. A child requires a loving, reliable caregiver for healthy development. The work of John Bowlby and others on early attachment revolutionized how hospitals handled maternal-infant bonding immediately after birth. As a result, from the 1960s onward, hospitals have taken a more thoughtful approach to preventing childhood hospital trauma.[6] In my work with incarcerated individuals, a disruption in healthy attachment during childhood is a very common theme. Of course, mental health professionals understand that disorders resulting from impaired attachment are also determined by heredity and social factors that cannot be easily teased apart. In truth, this describes many phenomena in psychiatry, which is to be expected when dealing with the most complex and mystifying organ in the human body. Compared to other fields of medicine, psychiatry is relatively new, and despite impressive progress over the past several decades, there remain large scientific gaps wherein confusion may flourish. One misunderstood form of emotional suffering recognized in psychiatry has been called the schizoid personality. Mental health professionals are sometimes taught that such individuals are cold, aloof, and uninterested in relationships. This is a misunderstanding. It is not people that they avoid, but emotional intimacy, which they experience as intrusive, controlling, and at times even persecutory.[7]

Let us use the example of schizoid personality to call attention to the complexity and intensity of emotional suffering that so often goes overlooked due to our insistence that "legitimate" mental turmoil can only mean a complete loss of contact with reality. Here I invite the reader to employ "forensic empathy" — the technique of putting oneself fully and nonjudgmentally inside the mind of the subject. Consider the inner pain of the schizoid individual. He or she is trapped in an excruciating dilemma of sensitivity and hunger for meaningful intimacy versus a fear of humiliation and exploitation by other's emotions. Social engagement is desperately needed, yet this desire is threatening and panic-inducing. Such individuals inevitably choose the only "reasonable" route available — isolation and inwardness. This type of suffering can be seen in ordinary persons, as well as intensely private intellectual and artistic geniuses such as Samuel Beckett, J. D. Salinger, and Franz Kafka.[8] It is a path that, followed too intently, leads to so much distance and inaccessibility that there can be no external checks on one's well-being.

The life mission of the individual laboring under a schizoid mindset is essentially carried out in a secluded isolation chamber, where the only self-validation is the echo of inner struggles. There may come a point where the only way out appears to be deeper isolation. This produces crippling loneliness and enhanced reliance on one's imagination — both of which must be paradoxically denigrated as signs of weakness, since they threaten one's illusion of absolute self-sufficiency and total logic. One becomes an enemy of one's self, yet needs this self for survival. It is an endgame with absolute zero on the horizon. All positive emotions and connections are extinguished, and the only thing to cling to in the face of an impending apocalypse is fidelity to one's ideals. Despite all uncompromising, dogged efforts to achieve a secure and safe haven, the outside world and reality will make itself known in due course. When it does, it will be felt as an intolerable invasion of one's sanctuary. In the throes of agonizing emotional deprivation, one may grasp for help from a last vestige of trust — one's family. Yet when family can neither comprehend the intensity of one's struggle, nor feel at ease with the presence of threatening inner torment, one must shut them out too while reeling from the sting of betrayal. One is then trapped with no escape, a fearful animal in a corner. At this point a preemptive strike becomes a rational strategy. If only someone would notice your fear and pain, lift you out of captivity and let you back into the wild, where at least you can continue searching the wilderness for sanctuary and freedom!

THE NEW ASYLUMS

Several years after my training with Dr. Resnick, I took the position of director of psychiatric services for the entire New Hampshire state prison system. I quickly found myself awash in human tragedy. Although I was initially motivated to study violence, I was overpowered by the suffering, despair, and tragic circumstances I encountered on a daily basis. One option for dealing with this was to form a hard callus over one's emotions and empathic capacity. But having been exposed to Buddhist psychology and my own personal psychoanalysis, I found myself unable to seriously consider this route. The only avenue open to me was staring more deeply into the suffering while attempting to make sense of it.

While I had the resources, finances, and professional connections to enjoy the services of a private, highly trained psychoanalyst, I was in the fortunate and privileged minority. Tragically, we have not had a functional mental health system in the United States for the past fifty years. No one bothered to create one that would survive deinstitutionalization. The number of mentally ill persons in jails and prisons began growing in the early 1970s as a result of what some have called "deinstitutionalization," which involved massive shutdowns of state hospitals. Correctional facilities then began to house persons with mental illness in record numbers, a phenomenon that came to be known as the "criminalization of the mentally ill."[9] Research conducted over the last several decades clearly shows that the rate of severe mental illness in corrections is four to eight times higher than in the general population.[10] Yet only 22 percent of state prisoners and 7 percent of jail inmates receive psychiatric treatment while incarcerated.[11] Correctional administrators have long recognized that their facilities are being used as dumping grounds for those better served through early psychiatric intervention — but the resources are simply not available. To be sure, there are those in prison whose mental illness is merely coincidental to their criminal behavior, just as there are those whose cardiovascular disease is coincidental to their decision to commit a crime.[12] But the sheer numbers of persons with serious mental illness in corrections as compared to the general population cannot be explained by so facile a theory as the mad/bad dichotomy, thus the situation demands a closer analysis.

States have continued to cut funding for mental health care, and more than 80 percent of states have fewer than the bare minimum number of psychiatric beds.[13] The incarceration of large numbers of mentally ill persons has led to the challenge of providing competent psychiatric care within facilities that are oriented primarily toward security and custodial care. In Virginia, jails house more persons with serious mental illness than Virginia psychiatric hospitals do.[14] The Los Angeles correctional system has been referred to as America's largest psychiatric facility.[15] The same can now be said for Chicago, and even the city where I now live — Syracuse. The disturbing reality is that American jails are now the primary venue for providing acute psychiatric inpatient treatment.[16] Caring for seriously mentally ill persons in corrections places a significant financial burden on state government and is a poor long-term financial strategy.[17] Nevertheless, until adequate community resources, additional psychiatric beds, and innovative alternatives are established, mental health services in corrections will remain a pressing and obligatory duty. How is the duty ensured? Presently, through costly and time consuming litigation.[18]

Inside U.S. jails and prisons, the mental health system is being "re-created," at substantial cost and effort, to treat the burgeoning number of seriously mentally ill persons. To date, there is no legal mechanism that serves to substantively reduce the number of persons with mental illness from entering the correctional system. By contrast, law enforcement agencies are armed with broad, often unreviewable, discretion in determining the destination (jail versus hospital) of arrestees suffering from mental illness. Laudable efforts have been made to divert seriously mentally ill persons away from corrections (e.g., jail diversion and mental health courts), yet their effectiveness is unclear, and they cannot keep pace. At present the trend shows no signs of reversing itself.

Over a decade ago, an American Psychiatric Association president put it about as plainly as one can: "A reasonable person could not fail to see the correlation among decreased funding for mental health resources, the closure of hospital beds, and homelessness and criminalization."[19] "Transinstitutionalization," the shift from mental health services to prison spending, has been the subject of academic and public discourse for quite a few decades. The theory underlying transinstitutionalization was published over seventy years ago. According to Penrose's Law (circa 1939), there will be a relatively stable number of persons confined in prisons and mental hospitals in any industrialized society.[20] If the population of one is reduced, the other will increase to compensate — sort of like squeezing a balloon on one end and having the other end get bigger. It appears that Penrose's Law is still applicable, and not just in the United States: other countries too are finding that as the number of psychiatric hospital beds is reduced, the number of people in prison rises.

In my role as a psychiatrist treating patients in the correctional and forensic system, I have witnessed innumerable tragedies resulting from our nonsystem of mental health: unnecessary deaths, suicides, and many thousands suffering from mental illness who found themselves called "inmate-patients" in the "New Asylums."[21] Looking deeper into this chasm, one finds another, even more unsettling trend. The relegation of psychiatry to the criminal justice system is not confined to adult mental health. Child psychiatrists now find themselves wondering whether "the national crisis in child community mental health services" is "contributing to delinquency and causing the juvenile justice system to become the dumping ground for youth who are inadequately served."[22] What makes this trend so disturbing (besides the loss of important youth mental health resources) is that it is occurring at a time when the juvenile justice system is losing its rehabilitative focus and becoming more punitive.

Stepping back and taking stock, it becomes difficult to escape the conclusion that society equates mental illness with criminality, danger, and violence. But even if one were to assume a direct association between violence against others and serious mental illness, the overall contribution of severely mentally ill persons to violent crimes is only about 3 percent.[23] When gun violence is considered, the percentage drops even lower. Further, in the absence of substance abuse, there is no significant relationship at all between psychiatric disorders and firearm violence.[24] Research in behavioral science has progressed to the point that we have a much better grasp of the clinical risk factors associated with violence and how to manage them. Such concerning risk factors are present in a small fraction of persons with serious mental illness, and they include acute psychosis, noncompliance with treatment, substance use, past violent behavior, and persecutory delusions.[25] But focusing broadly on all persons with mental illness as a "risky" population can be analogized to the unwarranted panic observed after 9-11, when anyone of Middle Eastern ancestry was viewed with heightened suspicion. It is not only a form of hysteria, but also slows progress in the treatment of mental illness by keeping it hidden and stigmatized.

The term "stigma" is synonymous with shame, disgrace, and humiliation. To stigmatize means to brand, slur, or defame. The term was rediscovered to an extent in the 1960s by famed sociologist Irving Goffman, who noted that "stigma is a process by which *the reaction of others spoils normal identity* [emphasis added]."[26] Thus, a social stigma, at its core, is the spoiling of the identity of certain persons, resulting in their alienated, exiled status. A powerful literary example of this is seen in Kafka's famous story "The Metamorphosis," which explores not only alienation, but also the profound betrayal that accompanies it. The main character, Gregor, wakes up one morning to discover that he has turned into a "monstrous vermin." The analogies with mental illness in the story are notable. Even Gregor's own family responds to him with horror and shuns him. Gregor's existence is transformed into an exercise of tolerating fear, isolation, and betrayal. At one point, his boss has an instinctive reaction on seeing Gregor: "His hand pressed over his open mouth, slowly backing away, as if repulsed by an invisible, unrelenting force."[27] His family shuts him away in a room, forgets him, and leaves him to die. Why, after so many years, do we continue to stigmatize mental illness? Part of the reason is deeply historical in its roots. The primitive notion that evil and mental illness are overlapping, related phenomena has been consistently perpetuated by the media and Hollywood movies. The ancient belief that evil is somehow involved in the origin of mental disease lingers in the shadows, and awaits resurrection in the wake of rare, horrific tragedies.

One such example of a rare, horrific tragedy occurred on December 14, 2012, when twenty-year-old Adam Lanza shot and killed his mother, then went on to shoot twenty children and six adults at the Sandy Hook Elementary school. Lanza then committed suicide by shooting himself. Shortly after the Sandy Hook tragedy, a senator announced that he supported measures to keep guns "out of the hands of criminals and the mentally ill."[28] This was followed by a national press conference in which the National Rifle Association vice president stated that "our society is populated by an unknown number of genuine monsters. People that are so deranged, so evil, so possessed by voices and driven by demons, that no sane person can even possibly comprehend them. . . . How can we possibly even guess how many, given our nation's refusal to create an active national database of the mentally ill?"[29] Such statements, widely disseminated by the media, merely reinforce the presumptive association between "criminals," "evil," and "the mentally ill." The sad and sobering fact is that the misguided association needs no further reinforcement. Research has clearly shown that there remains a strong stereotype of dangerousness and desire for social distance from those suffering from mental illness.[30] And somehow the irrationality has increased over time. A comparison of the research from 1950 and 1996 showed that perceptions of persons with mental illness as violent or frightening have not decreased; rather, they have *substantially increased*. In short, persons with serious mental illness are more feared today than they were half a century ago.[31]

Where is the outrage? Why isn't resolving the problem of criminalizing persons with mental illness the top priority of the American Psychiatric Association? (I suspect it is hidden behind a wall of emotional and political suppression, since immersing oneself in the U.S. correctional system is more than most can tolerate.)[32] The research results allow us to make some general assumptions about society's current beliefs about mental illness.[33] The beliefs may be paraphrased as follows: *People with mental illness are dangerous and unpredictable,* and *People with mental illness are not welcome in free society.*[34] It becomes hard to escape the conclusion, as suggested by the research on public beliefs, that society's primary motivation is to achieve social distance from individuals with serious mental illness. But where to banish unwanted persons? The "asylums" of a bygone era, now closed or demolished, are no longer a viable option. The remaining options would appear to be banishment to the streets (homelessness) and correctional institutions. We have reached an age in which we no longer see it as acceptable to execute persons with intellectual disabilities.[35] Thus one hopes that we might be proceeding toward an era in which this enlightenment may extend to declining to use prisons as our de facto mental health system.

Creation of a legitimate mental health system will take place incrementally based on our efforts, or not at all based on our complacency.

Moreover, no change will come without more reliable and effective treatments for psychiatric disorders. The indistinct shadows concealing mental illness must be dissolved by the light of demonstrable, as well as practical medical science. Only then will there be hope for reducing societal stigma, fear, and unseemly projections. Only then will mental illness be taken as the serious public health issue that it is. And only then will it be removed from the places where we send people for punishment, and returned to the healing attendance of the mental health profession.

MODERN MASS SHOOTINGS AND MASS DISTRACTION

Lately mass shootings continue to stir the debate about mental illness and violence. Despite enhanced media coverage, mass shootings by people with serious mental illness remain exceedingly rare events and represent a fraction of a percent of all yearly gun-related homicides. This should be contrasted to firearm deaths by suicide, which account for the majority of yearly gun-related deaths. The most recent research suggests that although the incidence may be increasing in recent years, there is an average of only 11.4 mass shooting incidents per year,[36] making these tragedies exceptionally hard to anticipate and avert.[37] The problem of mass shootings and the motives of the shooters in present-day society stand apart from mental illness generally. The recent phenomenon of mass shootings in the United States results from a combination of factors, including sociocultural ones that must be understood clearly if these rare and horrific tragedies are to be prevented. Investigating sociocultural factors in Western society requires considering the issues of narcissism and media responsibility. Narcissism may be considered the classic American pathology, but there is concern that it may be proliferating "virally" and gaining momentum.[38] Is the changing character of mass shootings over the past few decades the product, in part, of our increasingly narcissistic values?

In *The Narcissism Epidemic*, Twenge and Campbell note that while crime has dropped overall since the 1990s due to a variety of factors, crimes related to narcissism (or a wounded ego) are directly relevant to mass shootings. Harvard psychologist Steven Pinker laid out an impressive overview of how violence among *Homo sapiens* has greatly declined over the centuries due to a "civilizing process."[39] Pinker now wonders if we might have reached a point of limited returns. The harder-to-achieve gains may arguably lie in the realm of attenuating the problem of narcissism. Twenge and Campbell note that "narcissism and social rejection were two risk factors that worked together to cause aggressive behavior," and these have certainly been described in the histories of mass shooters.[40] They conclude, "Given the upswing in the narcissistic values of American culture since the 90s, it may be no coincidence" that mass shootings became a prominent concern around this time.

I have often wondered whether extensive media attention in the '90s may have propagated a Western "script," resulting in a perverse glamorization of the act—particularly in the eyes of subsequent perpetrators.[41] Consider the highly popular song "Jeremy" by the American rock band Pearl Jam, released in 1991. It reached the top five on Billboard charts, is still heard regularly on radio stations, and was inspired by a high school student who killed himself in front of his classmates. Like most popular songs of an age, it is simply a reflection of sentiments prevalent at the time: "Clearly I remember / Pickin' on the boy . . . But we unleashed a lion . . . Jeremy spoke in class today . . . Try to forget this, / Try to erase this / From the blackboard."

The study of individual cases of mass shootings that have occurred since the '90s suggest that perpetrators often felt socially rejected, and perceived society as continually denouncing them as unnecessary, ineffectual, and pathetic. To use a schoolyard metaphor, they are the kid always picked last for the sports team. Instead of bearing the burden of the humiliation in the multitude of ways that schoolchildren do, they plan a surprise attack to prove their hidden "value." They become martyrs of the excommunicated—too egotistic to surrender to and benefit from what they cannot accept about themselves. The very public, dramatic, and perhaps theatrical nature of mass murder seems to speak clearly to a "need for recognition from an audience."[42] The staged and exposed act of revenge has the function of establishing a connection with spectators who will not soon forget what they have seen. Western culture has constructed a vast and powerfully influential religion devoted to celebrity and fame. We now hold celebrity up as the single greatest achievement in life—one that should be attained at all costs. In place of what should be profound shame, there appears to be an aura of undeserved notoriety and infamy accorded to certain individuals who proclaim by deed: "I carry profound hurt—I'll go ballistic and transfer it onto you." News media have always been in the business of searching for "the right sort of madness" to capture the public's imagination.[43] This may involve exploiting violent and tragic acts and/or overemphasizing the alleged role of serious mental illness. The end result is that these tragedies can now "be evoked from the nation's collective memory in a word or two"—"Columbine" or "Virginia Tech."[44]

This Western cultural script is more clearly seen as a violent death parade celebrating infamy, in a bid for what Western culture prizes the most—*celebrity by any means necessary*. These sociocultural factors have been significantly amplified by the Internet and social media. The use of YouTube and other Internet platforms represents an attractive stage and sanctuary for individuals trapped by their conflicting needs for social attachment. Will the isolating virtual socialization of the Internet serve to worsen matters or ultimately provide a solution? For alienated, angry, vengeful individuals, their future and the future of their victims hang in the balance. Yet I have some fear that the Internet's virtual connectedness will only perpetuate the alienated loner's conflict: his wish for social connection versus his deep-seated mistrust. The *pretense* of genuine connections can be sustained well into young adulthood, leaving the individual without real experience in developing healthy social attachments. Such individuals will eventually awaken to the reality of their isolation. This will lead to feelings of being unwanted. And as Christian Schüle has written, "whoever is not needed is not a full member of society. Whoever feels this could run amok. In his blind rage at a wasted life, a person running amok sensationally highlights a functionally civilized society's most extreme recourse to its archetypal reflexes: in the martial pose of the victor, the individual takes revenge for the community's apparent failure to devote attention to him and acknowledge his self-worth."[45]

The final written communication of a recent mass shooter from California is entirely consistent with this pattern of alienation and malignant envy—culminating in a violent bid for fame and validation: "Humanity has rejected me. . . . Exacting my Retribution is my way of proving my true worth to the world."[46]

KINDLING A LIGHT

As far as we can discern, the sole purpose of human existence
is to kindle a light in the darkness of mere being.
—Carl Jung, *Memories, Dreams, Reflections*

I first met David in 2012, when I served as program chair for the Forty-Third Annual Meeting of the American Academy of Psychiatry and the Law (AAPL). I was in a position to recommend any keynote speaker I chose. A former trainee of mine had seen David Kaczynski speak and highly recommended him. David seemed like an excellent choice to me, not only because of all he had been through, but also because of all he had done for others. (I later learned about his countless speaking engagements advocating for improved mental health treatment, his anti–death penalty work and having helped run a shelter for runaway youth.) But in truth, I suppose my path to meeting David began much earlier, as a boy who was often preoccupied with violence and death.

When I was a boy about ten years old, I saw something that would stick in my memory for the rest of my life. It was a *Time* magazine cover. At the center was a large vat of Kool-Aid. Surrounding the vat were some nine hundred dead bodies. I'm not sure if it was that I was unable to process what it meant, or perhaps that I could process it only too well—the mind of a child is so open and honest. Regardless, I fixated on it. Later my schoolteacher gave us the assignment of writing a short story. While other children were writing stories about sports figures or the family pet, I was busy crafting an attempt to fathom something dreadful. In my story, I was a Jonestown member who managed to escape by feigning death. I can only speculate on my teacher's reaction to my work. If it signaled the need for a concerned parent-teacher conference, I was not included. Retrospectively, I am inclined to wonder whether this was an early warning sign that I might become a forensic psychiatrist. (About twenty years later, I would interview and become friends with one of the few living survivors of the Jonestown tragedy, who then lectured with me at a national conference.)[47] Since then, I always carried with me a teasing, mocking question: *Can you find the beauty in absolute ugliness?*

Much of my career—as a physician and later as a forensic psychiatrist—has been focused on similar themes: violence and death have been a daily focus of my concern. I come from two generations of physicians, and my family lost several patriarchs at an early age—one from mental illness and suicide. An ancient Zen Buddhist–influenced text advises that "meditation on inevitable death should be performed daily."[48] After my mother died at an early age from progressive multiple sclerosis, I found that meditation on death became an unavoidable condition. Through psychotherapy, meditation, and assistance from those wiser than me, insights came over time. I believe my family chose a field that concerns itself with trying to see death coming, prepare for it, and, if possible, stave it off. But of course, this is an illusion. Having discovered this, I shifted my focus to the ways in which our denial of death creates virtually all of our suffering.[49, 50, 51] I chose to go into the medical discipline that deals with the mind. Since Buddhists have been studying the mind for some twenty-five hundred years, its philosophy and psychology have much to offer. Through the study of both psychiatry and Buddhism, it became apparent to me that two of the mind's greatest foes are fear and a powerful pull to value one's self, even at the expense of peace and gratitude.

In 2012, I readied myself to introduce David's talk at AAPL in front of the country's leading forensic psychiatrists. At what is usually a stiff, formal setting, I immediately felt a sense of calm sincerity and kindness on meeting David. When the time came for me to introduce David, I set aside my prepared introduction and spoke from the heart. I introduced him as a "humanitarian, poet, and Buddhist." After David's talk and the extended standing ovation that followed, many colleagues approached me to say it was the best talk they had ever heard at AAPL. Another pulled me aside to tell me: "He radiates compassion."

A TRIP TO SANDY HOOK

I was pleasantly surprised by a thoughtful series of e-mail exchanges with David in November 2012. On December 14, 2012, and the days that followed, I was busy avoiding news media requests and keeping my children from watching the nonstop coverage out of Newtown, Connecticut. Then David contacted me again to see if I would be interested in joining him and two Buddhist teachers to speak as a part of the Sandy Hook Promise. I agreed without a moment's hesitation. Part of the mission of the Sandy Hook Promise is to have an open dialogue on all the relevant issues, a dialogue that includes various and opposing views. David had been invited by Sandy Hook Promise leaders to give a presentation titled "Violence, Loss and Emotional Healing: A Buddhist Perspective."[52]

The goal of our presentation was to explore the commonalities of mindfulness, Buddhism, and psychiatry as they applied to healing after severe trauma. I viewed my role as primarily to support, listen, and provide some basic information about "psychiatric first aid" in the immediate wake of mass trauma. Both expert consensus and common sense suggest that community support improves well-being in the wake of a mass tragedy, and the formation of the Sandy Hook Promise plainly suggested that this community understood what they needed to do.[53] I spoke about how mass trauma survivors appear to cope early on by cultivating (1) a sense of safety, (2) a sense of calm, (3) a sense of personal and community efficacy, (4) feelings of social connectedness, and (5) a realistic sense of optimism.

Indeed, these key coping efforts had been demonstrated by the Norwegian community not even a year and a half before the Sandy Hook tragedy. On July 22, 2011, Norway experienced immeasurable loss and trauma when a lone, angry individual named Anders Behring Breivik killed over seventy innocent people in a meticulously planned attack. Many of the victims were young teenagers attending a Youth League event. Immediately afterward, there was a remarkable and courageous response, much like that of Newtown.[54] The posttragedy reflections of the medical first responders were focused on collective responses of "strong engagement and feelings of togetherness."[55] It was very important to them at the time "to be compassionate and caring," in addition to enduring "the pain of others, without having a solution."[56] The Norwegian psychiatric professionals understood clearly how to assist with the early signs of acute stress and unbearable grief. In particular, they knew that one of their most valuable contributions would be "to listen," and help survivors "find new strength and meaning in a changed life."[57]

Several years after the mass tragedy in Norway, I would have the chance to study and lecture with the Norwegian forensic psychiatrist who performed the second forensic evaluation of the perpetrator, finding that he did not meet the Norwegian standards for the insanity defense.[58] It was a unique opportunity to study the mind of a mass murderer who lived after the incident, since many intend to die after carrying out the massacre. Breivik had published his own "manifesto," revealing his motivations as anti-Muslim and hoping to incite a revolt against multiculturalism. His writing of over fifteen hundred pages was titled *2083 a European Declaration of Independence* and was disseminated via e-mail some three hours before his massacre. Confirming how today's mass murderers can be influenced by their predecessors, Breivik heavily plagiarized Ted Kaczynski's *Industrial Society and Its Future*, deleting and inserting key words to promote his own agenda. Breivik turned himself in immediately after his massacre, and Norway witnessed an unprecedented criminal trial. After the first round of experts concluded he suffered from paranoid schizophrenia, a second round of expert evaluation was ordered. The second experts diagnosed Breivik with narcissistic personality disorder. Much of the debate focused on whether Breivik's self-centered grandiosity arose to the level of a delusion. Ultimately, he was found not to meet Norway's standard for the defense of not guilty by reason of insanity; he is currently serving twenty-one years in prison (the maximum penalty in Norway). Unsurprisingly, Breivik proclaimed he did not recognize the legitimacy of the court or its decision.

The strength and awe-inspiring resilience I witnessed during the Sandy Hook Promise presentation humbled me. In particular, I noticed how the people of Newtown made it clear that they *did not* want to be viewed as helpless victims. The Newtown community had known from the beginning what they needed to do, and they were well along the path toward establishing a sense of efficacy and optimism. The audience asked thoughtful questions about how best to reach out to show support for families of victims, and — in an overwhelming display of compassion — to the family members of the offender. Here David spoke with great authority and empathy. The Newtown audience knew that they had before them the person who was best equipped to answer this question, and they wanted to seize the moment. David spoke in his usual eloquent, humanistic, and compelling style. He concluded his insightful answer by saying: "We will always love our family members, but we detest what they did."

POSTTRAUMA REFLECTIONS

Until you've eaten with a chimp and bathed with a chimp,
you don't know a chimp.
—Sandra Herold, owner of Travis the Chimp

The synagogue where our Sandy Hook Promise talk was held was packed to standing room only. Just before taking our seats on the stage, we were informed by a community leader that "things were still raw." The statement felt less like a warning, and more like a protective blessing bestowed upon us. After we had given our talks, there was time for audience questions and comments. A man in the audience whom I imagined to be a Newtown father/brother/uncle/Little League coach stood up to ask the question I feared but knew was coming. He spoke calmly, but looked pained: "I need to ask this question of the doctor." And then he asked it, the question all of us wanted the answer to: "How could someone do what he did—to the little children?"

This was the question only Adam Lanza could definitively answer. But now the most relevant data was irretrievable. I wanted to give the man in the audience an answer that would both solve the puzzle and alleviate suffering. I felt the strong pull of answers that would have relieved my discomfort. I could oversimplify by raising the specter of "evil." I could give a detached recitation on the bio-psycho-social underpinnings of human violence. The gravity of the moment flattened all intellectual and academic explanations. Taking a measured breath, and channeling some of David's open-hearted sincerity, I summoned the most honest answer I could: "Sometimes . . . anger can be so intense that it can become blinding." There was a pause, and I feared my answer was not enough. I had held back due to my wish to say something that would facilitate healing. I had held back out of fear that anything I might say about Adam Lanza would come across as excusing his actions. Months later, I began to research the Lanza case in the same fashion I had analyzed other mass shootings. As usual, in retrospect, the familiar progression was there waiting to be uncovered. On December 20, 2011, Adam Lanza called a radio show to speak about a domesticated chimpanzee named Travis. Travis unexpectedly attacked his owner's friend in a horrific manner and was killed by police. Adam said to the radio host:

> When we see a chimp in that position, we immediately know that there's something profoundly wrong with the situation. And it's easy to say there's something wrong with it simply because it's a chimp, but what's the real difference between us and our closest relatives?
>
> Travis wasn't an untamed monster at all. . . . He *was* civilized. . . . Look what civilization did to him. . . .
>
> And his attack wasn't simply because he was a senselessly violent, impulsive chimp. . . . The best reason I can think of . . . would be that . . . he was overwhelmed at the life that he had, and he wanted to get out of it by changing his environment. . . . I just — just don't think it would be such a stretch to say that he very well could have been a teenage mall shooter or something like that.

Around the time of his radio show call, Adam Lanza made several posts on a popular Internet thread titled "You know what I hate?" He wrote:

> Culture. I've been pissed out of my mind all night thinking about it. I should have been born a chimp. . . .
>
> Now I've calmed down and am left lying on the floor, numbly perplexed over the foreign concept of loving life.

The Buddhist tradition teaches that meditation is a practice one must become familiar with to train one's mind. More importantly, it is a practice that should ultimately be realized in one's daily life, not just while sitting on a cushion. When the current of the mind whisks us away, we notice this, and then return to the present. This pattern is an eternal recurrence in both our minds and our lives. Repeatedly, we are hit by both small waves and devastating tsunamis. The practice of bringing ourselves back to life trains the mind to return to a state of equanimity. We are reborn into the present, over and over. On December 14, 2012, Adam Lanza committed mass murder and suicide. Days later, a group from the Newtown community formed the Sandy Hook Promise organization. Their Sandy Hook Promise states: "Our hearts are broken, but our spirit is not." With their hearts broken, they turned toward their spirit. And for the benefit of others, they started again.

How might we as a society learn from these tragedies? We think far too shallowly about these events. We concern ourselves with metal detectors, "profiles," and preventing "the mentally ill" from obtaining firearms. It is time we thought deeper, cultivating respect for how to teach compassion and personal responsibility in individual minds. These tragedies invite us to take a more substantive, meaningful look at how we view psychological suffering and violence as a species. They call us not only to reform our mental health system, but also to face ourselves with an open and fearless heart. The fearless and open heart searches for happiness, yet is willing to let go of pain, frustration, and that which it cannot get or avoid. An open and fearless heart seeks to take responsibility for its own anger. It does so by learning how not to externalize blame, by being willing to examine itself, and by cultivating responsibility. In the final analysis, no matter "what social or biological factors are involved, ultimately we must take responsibility for our anger."[59]

Mental and emotional turmoil occurs in us all. It is the elephant in the room that must be denied lest one be accused of seeing elephants. How seriously do we want to study and understand the mind? It is no trivial claim that our very future as a species depends on it. At what point will we begin to honor the vital importance of the mind, its awesome power and its infinite possibilities? To do so we must devote sufficient attention, time, and resources. Given what we currently understand about biology, the psychology of personality styles, and social influences, is it an unthinkable stretch to consider the following? Take an individual endowed with exquisite sensitivity, high intelligence, and a paradoxical nature (distant yet sensitive, aloof yet easily hurt). Might such a person be influenced by an incremental convergence of early trauma, intense parental expectations, and then teenage trauma resulting in profound existential confusion? Continuing forward cautiously, is it too fantastic a supposition that this individual might come to view human intimacy as oversocialization? If so, this person may well view intimacy as a serious cruelty and destruction of personal freedom. Alone and with time to think, this person might begin to ruminate about how the system of socialization results in unforgivable sacrifices.

The problem is that all of the foregoing is far too speculative. Furthermore, this line of thought is so taxing to one's mental economy that a more expeditious substitute is required.[60] One time-tested, undemanding route is to declare such an individual evil. But doing this still leaves one with the nagging problem of how the person "became that way" in the first place.[61] Moreover, declaring someone evil instantly summons the supernatural and mythological, leading us further away from rational thought. The real causes of violent behavior will always be different from the way people think of evil, because evil is defined through myth and illusion. This has been termed the "myth of pure evil" by a social psychologist who notes that "the face of evil is no one's real face—it is always a false image that is imposed or projected on the opponent."[62] Another hurdle to a better understanding of human violence is that our desire to know the "face of evil" battles with our desire to keep it partially obscured. The latter is necessary for keeping it the repository of unpleasant projections. Indeed, "humanizing" a monster "makes him less compelling as the embodiment of evil."[63] The celebrity status of serial killers in American culture reflects precisely such contradictory desires.[64] There is also the comforting conclusion that the killer is an "alien" aberration whose detection has made society a much safer place. The tendency to keep evil obscured is consistent with lay notions that evil is beyond comprehension and that those who commit evil acts lie outside the demarcation of being human.[65] Ultimately psychiatric researchers and clinicians cannot succumb to the myth of evil, since it will have the pernicious effect of shutting down scientific progress and treatment efforts.[66]

If we choose to be serious about treatment efforts, there can be no avoiding the reality that mental illness affecting the individual will invariably have an impact on family members. The experience of the family struggling to help a loved one with mental illness deserves much more attention than it has been given to date. Although the ordeal David and his family have suffered is an extreme one, I have no doubt that legions of families will be able to relate. Every day in America, families are challenged by the torturous hardship of ensuring lifesaving mental health care for their loved ones. Many have been pushed beyond the brink of what the strongest family could be expected to handle. They face not only deep concern about getting effective treatment for their affected kin, but also fear and confusion about what they observe. In some cases, they may even fear for their loved one's safety—as well as their own.

Despite all this, family can be some of the strongest medicine, and there are a number of things that families can do to stack the odds in their favor.[67] For example, here are some recommendations from my colleague Dr. Lloyd Sederer (medical director of the New York State Office of Mental Health), who has substantial experience consulting with families struggling to help their loved one with mental illness:[68]

Don't go it alone.

Document observations that are concerning to you.

Learn the "mental health system" rules.

Seek family therapy if needed.

Understand that you are engaged in a marathon, not a sprint.

Not going it alone means be ready and willing to reach out. A group that is highly regarded and plays a critical role in supporting families is the National Alliance on Mental Illness (NAMI).[69] NAMI advocates for access to services, treatment, support, and research. There are hundreds of state NAMI organizations, with groups in communities across the country. Attending a NAMI meeting, one quickly gets the sense of a supportive community of family members ready to help each other. Many NAMI members have substantial experience with obtaining help and treatment resources in their locale and thus serve as invaluable advisers to those who are less experienced. Documenting observations has to do with noticing and writing down factual descriptions of a loved one's concerning behavior. This can be important because in the midst of a crisis, it may be difficult to provide authorities or doctors with the critical evidence they need to ensure treatment. Written documentation of objective data by a family member can serve as either evidence needed for hospitalization or important data establishing a proper diagnosis. Learning the mental health system and how it works allows one to be a better advocate for a loved one in need of treatment. Often NAMI and other NAMI members can assist with this. In addition, a trusted psychiatrist or mental health professional can provide important information about who to speak with and, just as important, the proper things to say to ensure treatment.

The family working to help their loved one should view the process as a long-term one that is unlikely to have a quick resolution. There will most likely be setbacks, periods of despair, and serious testing of family morale. In a family system, one person often represents the "hub" of the family wheel. Traditionally this hub has been the mother, but it may be any other grounding, stabilizing personality. The hub keeps the family centered and on track. Should the hub disappear, the "spokes" of the family are vulnerable to flying apart, and the circle of the family is in jeopardy of breaking down. It is not uncommon that the person who represents the hub or heart of a family has an innate sense of when one of the spokes is seriously troubled. She may then find a way to communicate her concern to other family members. Indeed, she often knows which family member is best suited to be his brother's keeper. In other cases, it may be that the fear and turmoil that naturally accompanies the harrowing experience of coping with a seriously mentally ill loved one threatens to split the seams of family attachments. In such cases, family therapy may be of significant benefit and should be sought from an experienced and credentialed family therapist. The overarching view of family therapy considers the styles and systems of interactions in a family unit, which are crucial for the psychological health of all members.

Sometimes individuals with serious mental illness do not understand or believe that they are suffering from disturbing symptoms. All solicitations to consider treatment may be rejected, and any family member who expresses concerns about the need for treatment may be seen as a traitor or enemy. This dynamic often causes strain and distance between family members, threatening to split the family apart along its fault lines—be they past grievances, differing values, or unspoken loyalties. This is why families must remain cohesive and seek some way to bring disruptive emotional forces into the light of day. If those forces remain hidden, they will keep tearing the family apart; but if we can see them for what they are, we can address them directly and strengthen the bonds that have been under strain.

CODA

An event is not under its own power but depends on many present causes and conditions as well as many past causes and conditions. Otherwise, it could not come into being.
— His Holiness the Dalai Lama,
How to See Yourself as You Really Are

David came along at a time in my life when I desperately needed a real-life model of someone with an open and fearless heart. Over the past several years, David has graciously invited me to help teach in a series of workshops and retreats in which we work with survivors of trauma. I still get more out of the meetings than the attendees do. And so there you have it—the brother of the Unabomber is helping to heal the battle-scarred forensic psychiatrist who was exposed to his brother's case as a young trainee.

David Kaczynski—humanitarian, poet, Buddhist—is a consummate example of walking the path of the open and fearless heart. He did not turn away from the unfathomable fallout connected with his brother. Rather, he turned toward it, and then inward to find the courage to open his heart and help others. In doing so, he fully accepted responsibility. Acceptance of responsibility is an acquired skill that is cultivated by training the mind. An open heart means freedom and the mature ownership and control of our own thoughts, feelings, and actions. The steps to freedom lie within each individual, not in outer circumstances. It may be that this lesson is not widely taught in schools these days. Everyone wants freedom, yet freedom can remain only where there is skillful and appropriate restraint and responsibility. Here is our opportunity to walk the path of the fearless heart, as David has. It is possible to use these indescribably horrendous events to "either wake ourselves up or to put ourselves to sleep."[70] They represent the unacceptable to the absolute degree, but we must not turn away—only toward.

It seems to me a remarkable paradox that my initial journey into the heart of darkness, with intent to stare into the abyss, led to something I could never have predicted. It led to the brother of the Unabomber, one of the most compassionate and open-hearted people I've ever known, who taught me a lesson about how we are all interconnected. Hoping to find proof of beauty in absolute ugliness, I had become cynical. How wonderfully unexpected that it was David Kaczynski who finally taught me there is always the possibility of compassion, even in the darkest of places.

NOTES

1. J. Knoll and Phillip J. Resnick, "Master Educator," *Journal of the American Academy of Psychiatry and the Law* 35, no. 2 (2007): 154–157.
2. US v. Kaczynski 239 F. 3d 1108 — Court of Appeals, 9th Circuit, 2001.
3. Daniel Goleman, *Destructive Emotions: A Scientific Dialogue with the Dalai Lama* (New York: Bantam Dell, 2004).
4. B. Bodhi, "Reflections on the Fire Sermon," *Parabola* 37, no. 1 (2012): 11–17.
5. E. Wilson, *The Social Conquest of Earth* (New York: Liveright, 2013).
6. J. Bowlby and J. Robertson, "A Two-Year-Old Goes to Hospital," *Proceedings of the Royal Society of Medicine* 46, no. 6 (1953): 425–427.
7. J. Masterson and R. Klein, *Disorders of the Self: New Therapeutic Horizons: The Masterson Approach* (New York: Brunner/Mazel, 1995); N. McWilliams, *Psychoanalytic Diagnosis: Understanding Personality Structure in the Clinical Process*, 2nd ed. (New York: Guilford, 2011), chap. 9.
8. B. Simon, "Beckett's *Endgame* and the Abortion of Desire," in Simon, *Tragic Drama and the Family: Psychoanalytic Studies from Aeschylus to Beckett* (New Haven, CT: Yale University Press, 1993), chap. 7; see also Franz Kafka's *Letters to Milena* (New York: Shocken Books, 1990), especially "Alone I continue living, yet when a visitor arrives it kills me."
9. C. Quanbeck et al., "Mania and the Law in California: Understanding the Criminalization of the Mentally Ill," *American Journal of Psychiatry* 160 (July 2003): 1245–1250.
10. L. N. Robins and D. A. Reiger, eds., *Psychiatric Disorders in America: The Epidemiologic Catchment Area Study* (New York: Free Press, 1991); J. Rich, S. Wakeman, and S. Dickman, "Medicine and the Epidemic of Incarceration in the United States," *New England Journal of Medicine* 364, no. 22 (2011): 2081–2083.
11. D. J. James and L. E. Glaze, *Mental Health Problems of Prison and Jail Inmates* (Washington, DC: Bureau of Justice Statistics, 2006).
12. N. R. Gross and R. D. Morgan, "Understanding Persons with Mental Illness Who

Are and Are Not Criminal Justice Involved: A Comparison of Criminal Thinking and Psychiatric Symptoms," *Law and Human Behavior* 37, no. 3 (2013): 175–186; J. Baillargeon et al., "Psychiatric Disorders and Repeat Incarcerations: The Revolving Prison Door," *American Journal of Psychiatry* 166, no. 1 (2009): 103–109.

13. B. Kuehn, "Criminal Justice Becomes Front Line for Mental Health Care," *Journal of the American Medical Association* 311, no. 19 (2014): 1953–1954.

14. "State Trends: Jails Are Housing Majority of Mentally Ill," *Mental Health Law Reporter* 25, no. 10 (2007): 78.

15. E. Torrey and M. Zdanowicz, "Prison and Jails Are No Place for People with Mental Illness," *Idaho Statesman*, November 25, 2002, http://www.psychlaws.org /GeneralResources/article109.htm.

16. H. Lamb, L. Weinberger, J. Marsh, and B. Gross, "Treatment Prospects for Persons with Severe Mental Illness in an Urban County Jail," *Psychiatric Services* 58, no. 6 (2007): 782–786.

17. T. Kupers, *Prison Madness* (San Fransico: Jossey-Bass, Publishers, 1999).

18. J. Metzner, "Class Action Litigation in Correctional Psychiatry," *Journal of the American Academy of Psychiatry and the Law* 30 (2002): 19–29.

19. M. Goin, "Fiscal Fallout: Patients in the Criminal Justice System," *Psychiatric News* 38, no. 13 (2003): 3, 44.

20. L. Penrose, "Mental Disease and Crime: Outline of a Comparative Study of European Statistics," *British Journal of Medical Psychology* 18 (1939): 1–15.

21. E. Fuller Torrey, *Out of the Shadows: Confronting America's Mental Illness Crisis* (New York: John Wiley & Sons, 1997), excerpts at http://www.pbs.org/wgbh /pages/frontline/shows/asylums/special/excerpt.html (accessed March 30, 2015).

22. T. Grisso, "Do Childhood Mental Disorders Cause Adult Crime?," *American Journal of Psychiatry* 164, no. 11 (2007): 1625–1627.

23. S. Fazel and M. Grann, "The Population Impact of Severe Mental Illness on Violent Crime," *American Journal of Psychiatry* 163 (2006): 1397–1403, http://ajp .psychiatryonline.org/article.aspx?articleId=96905.

24. C. Martone et al., "Psychiatric Characteristics of Homicide Defendants," *American Journal of Psychiatry* 170 (2013): 994–1002.

25. J. Swanson et al., "A National Study of Violent Behavior in Persons with Schizophrenia," *Archives of General Psychiatry* 63, no. 5 (2006): 490–499; S. Ullrich, R. Keers, and J. Coid, "Delusions, Anger, and Serious Violence: New Findings from the MacArthur Violence Risk Assessment Study," *Schizophrenia Bulletin* 40, no. 5 (2013): 1174–1181; C. Webster, Q. Haque, and S. Hucker, *Violence Risk-Assessment and Management: Advances through Structured Professional Judgment and Sequential Redirections*, 2nd ed. (New York: Wiley-Blackwell, 2013); J. Coid et al., "The Relationship between Delusions and Violence: Findings from the East London First Episode Psychosis Study," *Journal of the American Medication Association Psychiatry* 70, no. 5 (2013): 465–471.

26. E. Goffman, *Stigma: Notes on the Management of Spoiled Identity* (New York: Prentice Hall, 1963).

27. F. Kafka, "The Metamorphosis," in *The Complete Stories*. Ed. N. Glatzer (New York: Shocken Books, 1971), 100.

28. Daniel Strauss, "Rubio Supports 'Comprehensive Study' of Gun Laws," *TheHill.com*, December 17, 2012, http://thehill.com/blogs/blog-briefing-room/news/273273-rubio-supports-comprehensive-study-of-gun-laws.

29. "Remarks from the NRA Press Conference on Sandy Hook School Shooting" (transcript), *Washington Post*, December 21, 2012, http://www.washingtonpost.com/politics/remarks-from-the-nra-press-conference-on-sandy-hook-school-shooting-delivered-on-dec-21-2012-transcript/2012/12/21/bd1841fe-4b88-11e2-a6a6-aabac85e8036_story.html.

30. B. G. Link, J. C. Phelan, M. Bresnahan, A. Stueve, and B. A. Pescosolido, "Public Conceptions of Mental Illness: Labels, Causes, Dangerousness, and Social Distance," *American Journal of Public Health* 89, no. 9 (1999): 1328–1333.

31. J. Phelan, B. Link, A. Stueve, and B. Pescosolido, "Public Conceptions of Mental Illness in 1950 and 1996: What Is Mental Illness and Is It to Be Feared?," *Journal of Health and Social Behavior* 41, no. 2 (June 2000): 188–207.

32. R. Ferguson, *Inferno: An Anatomy of American Punishment* (Cambridge, MA: Harvard University Press, 2014).

33. Portions of this discussion are adapted with permission from J. Knoll, "Fearful Synergy: Society and Psychiatry Perpetuating the Criminalization of the Mentally Ill," *Correctional Mental Health Report* 10, no. 1 (2008): 3–4, 12–16.

34. G. Bizer, J. Hart, and A. Jekogian, "Belief in a Just World and Social Dominance Orientation: Evidence for a Mediational Pathway Predicting Negative Attitudes and Discrimination against Individuals with Mental Illness," *Personality and Individual Differences* 52 (2012): 428–432; B. G. Link, J. C. Phelan, M. Bresnahan, A. Stueve, and B. A. Pescosolido, "Public Conceptions of Mental Illness: Labels, Causes, Dangerousness, and Social Distance," *American Journal of Public Health* 89, no. 9 (1999): 1328–1333.

35. See *Atkins v. Virginia*, 536 S. Ct. 304 (2002), and *Hall v. Florida*, 134 S. Ct. 1986 (2014).

36. J. Blair and K. Schweit, *A Study of Active Shooter Incidents, 2000–2013* (Washington, DC: Texas State University and Federal Bureau of Investigation, U.S. Department of Justice, 2014).

37. O. Saleva, H. Putkonen, O. Kiviruusu, and J. Lonquist, "Homicide-Suicide—An Event Hard to Prevent and Separate from Homicide or Suicide," *Forensic Science International* 166 (2007): 204–208.

38. J. Twenge and W. Campbell, *The Narcissism Epidemic: Living in the Age of Entitlement* (New York: Free Press, 2009).

39. S. Pinker, *The Better Angels of Our Nature: Why Violence Has Declined* (New York: Viking, 2011).

40. Twenge and Campbell, *The Narcissism Epidemic*.

41. P. Mullen, "The Autogenic (Self-Generated) Massacre," *Behavioral Sciences and the Law* 22 (2004): 311–323.

42. Y. Neuman, "On Revenge," *Psychoanalysis, Culture and Society* 17 (2012): 1–15.

43. J. Ronson, *The Psychopath Test: A Journey through the Madness Industry* (New York: Riverhead Books, 2011).

44. Associated Press, "Mass Public Shootings on the Rise, But Why?," April 21, 2007, http://www.nbcnews.com/id/18249724#.U7TIE9FOWUk.

45. C. Schüle, "Tokyo Subway Dreams: Underground Meditations," in *Tokyo Compression Three*, ed. M. Wolfe (Hong Kong: Asia One Books, 2012).

46. Elliot Rodger, "My Twisted World," available at https://www.documentcloud .org/documents/1173808-elliot-rodger-manifesto.html.

47. "Mass Murder and Mind Control: Understanding the Jonestown Tragedy," presentation at the annual meeting of the American Academy of Psychiatry and the Law, Miami, FL, October 20, 2007.

48. Y. Tsunetomo, *Hagakure: The Book of the Samurai*, trans. W. Wilson (Tokyo: Kodansha International, 1979).

49. E. Becker, *The Denial of Death* (New York: Free Press, 1973).

50. T. Pyszczynski, S. Sheldon, and J. Greenberg, *In the Wake of 9/11: The Psychology of Terror* (Washington, DC: American Psychological Association, 2006).

51. J. Schimel, J. Hayes, T. Williams, and J. Jahrig, "Is Death Really the Worm at the Core? Converging Evidence That Worldview Threat Increases Death-Thought Accessiblity," *Journal of Personality and Social Psychology* 92 (2007): 789–803.

52. "Violence, Loss and Emotional Healing: A Buddhist Perspective," March 13 at Adath Israel, *Newtown Bee*, March 1, 2013, http://newtownbee.com/news/news /2013/03/01/violence-loss-and-emotional-healing-buddhist-persp/6291.

53. S. Hobfoll et al., "Five Essential Elements of Immediate and Mid-Term Mass Trauma Intervention: Empirical Evidence," *Psychiatry* 70, no. 4 (2007): 283–315; A. M. Vicary and R. C. Fraley, "Student Reactions to the Shootings at Virginia Tech and Northern Illinois University: Does Sharing Grief and Support over the Internet Affect Recovery?," *Personality and Social Psychology Bulletin* 36, no. 11 (2010): 1555–1563.

54. S. Sollid, "When Worst Comes to Worst—the Long Road Home," *Tidsskrift for den norske legeforening* (*Journal of the Norwegian Medical Association*) 131 (2011): 1748.

55. F. Thrana, "Endure the Pain of Others," *Tidsskrift for den norske legeforening* (*Journal of the Norwegian Medical Association*) 131 (2011): 1747–1748.

56. C. Haug, "Reflections," *Tidsskrift for den norske legeforening* (*Journal of the Norwegian Medical Association*) 131 (2011): 1739.

57. G. Dyb, "Lean Forward and Be There," *Tidsskrift for den norske legeforening* (*Journal of the Norwegian Medical Association*) 131 (2011): 1751–1752.

58. C. Leonard, D. Annas, J. Knoll, and T. Terje Tørrissen, "The Case of Anders Behr-

ing Breivik—Language of a Lone Terrorist," *Behavioral Sciences and the Law* 32, no. 3 (2014): 408–422; and "Breivik: All-Consuming Hatred Approaching Psychosis?," copresented with Terje Torrissen, MD, at Forty-Fourth Annual Meeting of the American Academy of Psychiatry and the Law, San Diego, CA, October 25, 2013.

59. R. Leifer, *Vinegar into Honey* (Ithaca, NY: Snow Lion Press, 2008).

60. B. Masters, *The Evil That Men Do: From Saints to Serial Killers* (London: Black Swan, 1997).

61. L. Watson, *Dark Nature: A Natural History of Evil* (New York: HarperCollins, 1995).

62. R. Baumeister, *Evil: Inside Human Violence and Cruelty* (New York: Henry Holt and Company, 1997).

63. G. Gabbard, "Book review: *Hannibal*," *American Journal of Psychiatry* 156, no. 11 (1999): 2001.

64. D. Schmid, *Natural Born Celebrities: Serial Killers in American Culture* (Chicago: University of Chicago Press, 2005).

65. T. Mason, J. Richman, and D. Mercer, "The Influence of Evil on Forensic Clinical Practice," *International Journal of Mental Health Nursing* 11 (2002): 80–93.

66. J. Knoll, "The Recurrence of an Illusion: The Concept of 'Evil' in Forensic Psychiatry," *Journal of the American Academy of Psychiatry and the Law* 36, no. 1 (2008): 105–116.

67. L. Sederer, *The Family Guide to Mental Health Care* (New York: W. W. Norton, 2013).

68. L. Sederer, "When Mental Illness Enters the Family," TED Talk, 2014, January 6, 2015, https://www.youtube.com/watch?v=NR00-JXuFMY.

69. See http://www.nami.org/.

70. Pema Chodron, *When Things Fall Apart: Heart Advice for Difficult Times* (Boston: Shambhala, 2007).

ACKNOWLEDGMENTS

AN ABBREVIATED VERSION of the chapter "Missing Parts" was published in *Brothers: 26 Stories of Love and Rivalry*, ed. Andrew Blauner (Hoboken, NJ: Jossey-Bass, 2009).

An excerpt from "Missing Parts" titled "My Brother, Ted" appeared in *Playboy*.

I also want to thank several people whose help along the way has been crucial:

My editor, Gisela Fosado, without whose patience, encouragement, and tactful advice this book would not have materialized.

Dr. James Knoll, for his insight in connecting my family story with psychiatric research and our collective need to face societal challenges related to mental illness, stigma, anger, and violence.

The many people unmentioned in the book who nevertheless played key roles in preventing further loss of life, principally Susan

Swanson, Anthony Biscelglie, Quin Denvir, Judy Clarke, Gary So-wards, and Scharlette Holdman.

My four "brothers"—Joel Schwartz, Tim Bennett, Gary Wright, and Bill Babbitt—whose friendship sustained me through difficult times.

My life's blessing, Linda Patrik, who saved an untold number of lives.

INDEX